From Eden to Babel

From Eden to Babel

An Adventure in Bible Study

RICHARD D. NELSON

CHALICE
PRESS

ST. LOUIS, MISSOURI

Cover art: FotoSearch
Cover and interior design: Elizabeth Wright

Visit Chalice Press on the World Wide Web at
www.chalicepress.com

10 9 8 7 6 5 4 3 2 1   06 07 08 09 10 11

Library of Congress Cataloging–in–Publication Data

Nelson, Richard D. (Richard Donald), 1945-
   From Eden to Babel : an adventure in Bible study / Richard D. Nelson.
      p. cm.
   ISBN-13: 978-0-8272-1039-4 (pbk. : alk. paper)
   ISBN-10: 0-8272-1039-6 (pbk. : alk. paper)
   1. Bible. O.T. Genesis II-XI, 9—Commentaries. I. Title.
   BS1235.53.N45 2006
   222'.1106—dc22

                                                          2006006290

Printed in the United States of America

Contents

Abbreviations

JSOT	*Journal for the Study of the Old Testament*
JSOTSup	*Journal for the Study of the Old Testament* Supplement Series
KJV	*King James Version*
NAB	*New American Bible*
NJB	*New Jerusalem Bible*
NJPS	*New Jewish Publication Society Translation*
NRSV	*New Revised Standard Version*
REB	*Revised English Bible*
RSV	*Revised Standard Version*
SSN	*Studia semitica neerlandica*
VT	*Vetus Testamentum*

Hebrew Word List

(The words below italicized in parentheses give the basic Hebrew term beside its most frequent English translation. Indented under the main entry are the various translations the NRSV uses for the same Hebrew term in various contexts in Genesis; realizing the same Hebrew term is used helps you see the artistry, meaning, and structure the original author intended.)

animal (*běhemah*)
   cattle 2:20
   animals 3:14; 6:7
animal of the field (*ḥayyat haśśādeh*)
    animal of the field 2:19, 20
    wild animal 3:1
    wild creature 3:14
bear (*yālad*)
   bear 4:1, 2, 17, 18 ("was born"), 20, 22, 25, 26; 6:1, 4
   bring forth 3:16
   be the father of (with a man as subject) 4:18 (3x)
begin (*ḥālal*)
   begin 4:26; 6:1
   be the first to 9:20
   beginning 11:6
both (*šěnayîm*)
   both 2:25; 3:7; 9:23
   two 9:22
build (*bānah*)
   build 4:17; 11:4, 5, 8
   make 2:22
call (*qārāʾ*)
   call 2:19 (2x), 20, 23; 3:9
   with "name" as the object of the verb
     give names 2:20
     name 3:20; 4:17, 25, 26
     call 11:9
   invoke 4:26

meet 4:14
come upon 4:15; 11:2
forever (*ʿôlām*)
   forever 3:22; 6:3
   of old 6:4
give (*nātan*)
   give 3:6, 12 (2x)
   yield 4:12
go out (*yāṣāʾ*)
   flow out 2:10
   go away 4:16
   go out 9:18
good (*ṭôb*)
   good 2:9 (2x), 12, 17, 18; 3:5, 6, 22
   fair 6:2
ground (*ʾădāmah*)
   ground 2:5, 6, 7, 9, 19; 3:17, 19, 23; 4:2, 3, 10, 11, 12; 6:1
   soil 4:14; 9:20
   earth 6:7
head (*rōʾš*)
   branch 2:10
   head 3:15
   top 11:4
hear (*šāmaʿ*)
   hear 3:8, 10; 4:23
   listen to 3:17
   understand 11:7
heavens (*šāmayim*)
   heavens 2:4 (2x); 11:4
   [birds of the] air 2:19, 20; 6:7
keep (*šāmar*)
   keep 2:15; 4:9
   guard 3:24
kill (*hārag*)
   kill 4:8, 14, 15 ("whoever kills"), 23, 25
   in 4:15 a different verb is used for "would kill him"
live, in the sense of "dwell" (*šākan*)
   place 3:25 (= cause to dwell)
   live 9:27
living being (*nepeš ḥayyah*)
   living being 2:7

living creature 2:19
make (*ʿāśah*)
  make 2:4, 18; 3:1, 7, 21; 6:6, 7
  do 3:13, 14; 4:10
  three other Hebrew words are translated "make" in 2:22;
     4:22; and 11:3
  the verb is not present in 2:9; 3:6; 9:27; in these
     verses a special grammatical form expresses "make"
man, in the generic sense; the first male human being (*ʾādām*)
  man 2:7 (2x), 8, 15, 16, 18, 19 (2x), 20 (2x), 21, 22
     (2x), 23 ("the man said"), 25; 3:8, 9, 12, 17, 20, 21, 22,
     24; 4:1 ("the man knew")
  [no] one 2:5
  Adam 4:25
  people 6:1, 7
  mortals 6:3
  humans 6:4
  humankind 6:5, 6
  human beings 6:7
  "they" 6:2; more literal "the daughters of *ʾadam*"
man, in the sense of male human being (*ʾîš*)
  man 2:23, 24; 4:1 ("produced a man"), 23 ("killed a man");
  9:20
  husband 3:6, 16
  "warriors of renown," 6:4 more literal "men of renown"
  "they said to one another," 11:3; more literal "they said, each
     man to his neighbor"
  "not understand one another's speech," 11:7; more literal "not
     understand, each man his neighbor's speech"
midst (*tāwek*)
  midst 2:9
  middle 3:3
  among 3:8
  "in his tent," 9:21; more literal "in the midst of his tent"
name (*šem*)
  name 2:11, 13, 14, 19, 20; 4:19, 21, 26 ("invoke the name"); 11:4
  renown 6:4
  incorporated as an expression with the verb call (*qārāʾ*)
     name 3:20; 4:17, 25, 26
  call 11:9
  "named it Enoch after his son," 4:17; more literal "called the
     name of the city after the name of Enoch his son"

nostrils (*ʾap*) 2:7
  nostrils 2:7
  face 3:19
offspring, literally "seed" (*zeraʿ*)
  offspring 3:15
  child 4:25
  "your offspring and hers," 3:15; more literal "your seed and
      her seed"
one (*ʾeḥād*)
  one 2:21, 24; 3:22; 4:19; 11:1 ("one language")
  first 2:11
  same 11:1 ("same words")
pangs (*ʿiṣṣābôn*)
  pangs 3:16
  toil 3:17
[be] pleasant (*neḥmād*)
  be pleasant 2:9
  be desired 3:6
put (*śîm*)
  put 2:8; 4:15
  lay 9:23
  a different Hebrew word is translated "put" in 2:15
put (*šît*)
  put 3:15
  appointed 4:25
reach out (*šālaḥ*)
  reach out 3:22
  send forth 3:23
rule (*māšal*)
  rule 3:16
  master 4:7
see (*rāʾah*)
  see 2:19; 3:6; 6:2, 5; 9:22, 23; 11:5
  a different Hebrew word (*hēn*) is translated "see" in 3:22
settle (*yāšab*)
  settle 4:16; 11:2
  live in 4:20
son (*ben*)
  son 4:17, 25, 26; 6:2, 4; 9:18, 19, 24
  children 3:16
sound (*qôl*)
  sound 3:8, 10

INTRODUCTION

The Self-reliant Reader

This book is not really directed at ministers and other professional interpreters of the Bible, although I hope they will read it. Instead, I am writing for "amateur" Bible readers, self-reliant people who want to read the first stories of Genesis on their own and apply them to their own lives. I am writing for people who find the Bible fascinating and irresistible and want to appreciate and understand it on their own. After all, *amateur* is French for "one who loves."

If you have bought or borrowed this book, you are someone with a special interest in the Bible and its message. You may be a lay congregational leader or a teacher of adults or children. Perhaps you are simply curious and find yourself drawn to and puzzled by the fascinating stories in the first part of Genesis. There are plenty of puzzles in these stories, to be sure, but also attractions. When we encounter the first man and woman, the first murderer, the first angry avenger, the first drunk, or the ambitious city builders of Babel, we are likely to discover ourselves. We can see our own faces in the mirror of the biblical narrative, recognizing these characters as "bone of my bones / and flesh of my flesh" (Gen. 2:23). Like the fruit that Eve plucked from the tree, these stories are "a delight to the eyes" and "desired to make one wise" (3:6). Reading them in a serious manner has the potential to change us in unexpected ways.

Our ancestors usually owned only a few books, but the Bible was always one of them. Previous generations read the Bible on their own and aloud to their families. They learned passages by heart and interpreted what they read using their own intelligence and what they may have learned in church. Unfortunately, most Christians today are increasingly willing to leave the interpretation of the Bible completely in the hands of professionals—ministers, professors, and writers of commentaries and devotional books. There are special annotated Bibles for every demographic group and personal need. We need to ask ourselves whether turning the interpretation of the Bible entirely over to experts is a healthy development. The Reformers translated the Bible into the language of the common people because they believed that biblical interpretation was something that ordinary Christians could do without a lot of outside guidance.

As you encounter these ancient stories from Genesis, I hope that you will feel empowered to move beyond being merely passive consumers of the interpretations of others. On the other hand, no one should interpret the Bible in a vacuum, without paying attention to what other Christians think and have thought about it. Responsible biblical interpretation is not a do-it-yourself project. For one thing, both the Old and New Testaments originated long ago in cultures that had customs and ways of thinking very different from our own. Consequently, I will be providing you with plenty of background information and guidance as you work through these stories. However, the basic purpose of this book is to teach you how to read the Bible on your own as much as possible—carefully, independently, and responsibly. It will introduce you to interpretive methods that will help you discover, uncover, and recover meanings in biblical texts that make sense to you and that address issues and situations that you care about.

In earlier centuries, people learned to become cabinetmakers or printers or lawyers by serving an apprenticeship. In a sense, I am asking you to become apprentice interpreters, following me around and looking over my shoulder as we work on these stories together. The goal is for you to develop into self-assured and responsible readers of the Bible.

I ask two things of you. First, try to remain open-minded about what I have to say. Much will be new. Some things may sound outrageous or even irreverent. Perhaps in the end you will disagree with my perspectives and suggestions. That is great, in my opinion, as long as your judgments are based on your own careful reading of these stories and not on preconceived notions or prejudices. My second request is that you do the assignments that I set for you. Read the Bible slowly and carefully, and go through the "Steps in Interpretation" listed below for each text in turn. When I cite a biblical passage from somewhere else in Scripture, take the time to look it up and read it. Your investment in time and effort will be well worth it.

Steps in Interpretation

Here is a summary of the methodology you will practice as apprentice interpreters.

Read the text several times slowly and carefully until you are familiar with it. Then take each of the following interpretive steps in turn and examine the text with that task or question in mind. Always jot down your responses and thoughts. Force yourself to write something, even if it sounds obvious, inadequate, or silly! Writing your conclusions keeps you focused and prevents you from forgetting your insights. Keep at it until you come to some sort of answer for each task or question. Also, write down whatever puzzles or questions you may come up with. Sometimes you will have more mysteries and problems than clear and simple answers. This is good! The "hard places" may prove to be the cutting edge of the text's new and surprising word for you.

1. Bracket off what you think you already "know" about the text; read with an open mind.
2. What is familiar about the text? How are we like the first readers?
3. What is unfamiliar? What surprises, puzzles, or shocks you? How are we different from the first readers?
4. What are the key words—words that are repeated or pivotal to the text's movement and meaning?
5. What opposing or contrasting pairs of words or ideas are present?
6. What are the various characters like? What do they do? With whom does the text seem to encourage you to identify?
7. What patterns give structure to the language and movement of the text? Look for repeated words or phrases. Look for "envelopes" or "bookends," concentric structures, and wordplays. Analyze how pronouns are used and how characters are addressed.
8. Describe the movement of the plot. How does it move from initial problem to resolution? Can you draw a flow chart or a diagram of this? What parts move the story forward and what parts provide background or delay resolution?

9. What is the text's purpose or intention or goal? What is it designed to do to you as a reader; how does it affect or change you?
10. How does context shape how you read the text, and how does the text contribute to its own context?
11. What claims or assertions does the text make about humanity and the world? What kind of God does it describe? What does this God do and care about?

Sources

Two readable and liberating books about the early chapters of Genesis are Ellen van Wolde, *Stories of the Beginning: Genesis 1–11 and Other Creation Stories* (Harrisburg: Morehouse Press, 1997) and Robert F. Capon, *Genesis: The Movie* (Grand Rapids: Eerdmans, 2003). Timothy R. Carmody, *Reading the Bible: A Study Guide* (New York: Paulist Press, 2004) surveys the entire Bible and serves as a primer in biblical interpretation, giving the reader a chance to work on several texts.

Donald E. Gowan, *From Eden to Babel: A Commentary on the Book of Genesis 1–11,* International Theological Commentary (Grand Rapids: Eerdmans, 1988) is an easy-to-follow commentary, perfect for the nonspecialist. Shamai Gelander, *Literature and Theology in Genesis 1–11,* Studies in the History of Judaism 147 (Atlanta: Scholars Press, 1997) offers a more challenging approach using the tools of literary study. For a non-Western perspective on these chapters, see Modupe Oduyoye, *The Sons of God and the Daughters of Men: An Afro-Asiatic Interpretation of Genesis 1–11* (Maryknoll, N.Y.: Orbis Books, 1984).

Two important tools for the self-reliant interpreter are a Bible dictionary and a concordance keyed to the translation you are using. Two good examples of the former are *Eerdmans Dictionary of the Bible* (Grand Rapids: Eerdmans, 2000) and *The HarperCollins Bible Dictionary* (San Francisco: Harper San Francisco, 1996).

CHAPTER 1

Reading Old Stories with New Eyes

Stop right now! Instead of digging right into this chapter, I want you to find a Bible (a *New Revised Standard Version* if at all possible) and read Genesis 2:4–4:26; 6:1–8; 9:18–27; and 11:1–9 at least twice through. Once you have done this you are ready to start reading this book.

Close Reading

When you read Genesis 2–3, did you read it carefully enough to observe the following details?

- The first half of 2:15 repeats the content of the second half of 2:8.
- In 2:17 God threatens that disobedience will mean immediate death ("on the day"), but this does not happen.
- God made Snake and all animals as potential helpers (2:18–20; 3:1).
- Woman restates God's original prohibition to make it even stricter (2:17; 3:3).
- Snake doesn't exactly lie in 3:4–5. The humans do not die (immediately). Instead their eyes open up, they acquire new knowledge, and they become like God in some way (3:7, 22).
- Woman's evaluation of the tree agrees with much of what was said about all the trees (2:9; 3:6).

- In 2:9 the tree of life is described as being in the center of the garden, but Eve changes this to put the forbidden tree in the center (3:3).
- The story begins with "no one to till the ground" and finishes with provision made for people "to till the ground" (2:5; 3:23).
- God's placement of humanity in Eden and their expulsion from there are each narrated twice: 2:8 and 15; 3:23 and 24.

Please do not be worried if you didn't catch these details. The skill of slow, deliberate, and attentive reading takes time and effort to develop. Scholars call this "close reading." It lies behind all of the interpretive work we will be doing together. When you practice the interpretive tasks listed in "Steps in Interpretation" (in the Introduction), you will be practicing close reading. Responsible and fruitful interpretation requires that we read texts slowly and carefully several times through and write down points and questions that occur to us.

However, slow and careful reading can be a problem, because most of us have learned to read as quickly as we can. Indeed, to survive in the modern world we have to skim through much of the written material that confronts us: office paperwork, junk mail, the daily paper. Here are some tips to help you slow down and pay attention to every word on the page:

- Hold a ruler under the lines you read. Do not move it down to the next line until you feel you have really looked at the words in front of your eyes.
- As you read, underline one or two key words in each sentence.
- Read the text out loud to yourself. Reading aloud was the universal practice in the ancient world. It helps you discover patterns and connections between sentences and paragraphs.
- Write a short sentence summary for each paragraph.

Always read a text more than once, looking for different sorts of details each time. The first time through you might want to look for key words, ones that are repeated or critical to what the text is talking about. The next time through you might want to ask what is familiar or unfamiliar about the text. Perhaps in a third reading you could look at the various characters and what they do and say.

Encountering Genesis 2–11

The fascinating tales in Genesis 2–11 speak about human life, with all its tragedies and ambiguities. As these stories unfold from

Eden's garden to the tower of Babel, they explore some of the basic realities of what it means to be human: family life, sexuality, childbirth, work, conflict, violence, social oppression, ethnic divisions, and language differences.

For many of us, though, the stories that begin Genesis no longer seem to be helpful as resources for understanding our faith. Church leaders often avoid these chapters as dangerous ground because of the role these chapters play in debates between religion and science. There was a time when believers simply regarded the early parts of Genesis as sheer historical fact; and, of course, quite a few still do. However, today many faithful Christians are bothered by what they see as unscientific claims that humanity has only been on earth for a few thousand years or that we were literally molded out of dust by God's hands. Many Christians are pretty certain that Adam and Eve or Cain and Abel or Noah and his sons are not to be taken as literal, historical characters.

Another thing—the level of sex and violence in the stories of Genesis 2–11 suggests that they should be "adult rated"! Consider 4:23–24; 6:2; or 9:22, for example. Nonetheless, Christian educators and Sunday school teachers usually sanitize these chapters and then present them as nursery school stories with moral lessons. Don't disobey (Genesis 3). Be nice to your sisters and brothers (4:1–16). Don't be arrogant (11:1–9). Narratives with violent or antisocial overtones—such as Lamech's unrestrained vengeance (4:23–24), sex between human women and heavenly beings (6:1–4), or Noah's drunken nakedness resulting in Canaan's slavery (9:18–27)—are treated with caution or furtively ignored.

Moreover, we may be kept from taking these stories seriously because we have inherited negative presuppositions and prejudices about them. Don't they insist that sex is sinful and that women are inferior? What about so-called "original sin"? Isn't that unfair? Weren't the stories of Cain's mark and the curse on Ham's son Canaan once used to justify racism and slavery?

The familiar stories in Genesis 2–11 have traditionally been interpreted as cautionary episodes in the destructive history of human sin. The themes of human rebellion and divine punishment are clearly present, of course. Yet many other meanings and topics appear in these stories. Remarkably, it is those alternative viewpoints that often seem to be more intriguing, evocative, and relevant to our contemporary situation. For example, if we are willing to set aside thoughts of original sin and punishment, we can read Genesis 2–3 as a timeless story of how human beings have grown up. Adam and Eve move from innocent childhood as "babes in the wood" to sadder-but-wiser adulthood in a sort of "kindergarten of Eden."

In the chapters that follow Eden, violence explodes from the heart of the human family, driven by sibling antagonism and religious dispute (4:1–16). This violence snowballs into widespread bloodshed and collective retribution (4:17–26). Sexuality breaches the boundary between the proper sphere of human existence and forbidden realms of supernatural power (6:1–8). Ethnic division and oppression emerge (9:18–27). Misunderstanding and miscommunication lead to the failure of a monumental project in civic architecture, one that had been intended to proclaim human accomplishment and guarantee permanence and stability (11:1–9).

Why These Stories?

In chapters 2 through 5 we will cover Genesis 2:4–4:26 (Adam and Eve, Cain and Abel, Cain's descendants). Chapter 6 deals with Genesis 6:1–8 (sex between the sons of God and human women), and chapter 7 with 9:18–27 (Noah's curse on Canaan). Chapter 8 considers 11:1–9 (the Tower of Babel).

I have chosen these particular narratives chiefly because they portray human drama and interaction. They are genuinely interesting stories with characters, plots, and conflict. As such they are quite different from the majestic and repetitive actions of God in Genesis 1:1–2:4 or the genealogies of Genesis 5, 10, and 11:10–32.

We will not be looking at the flood story (6:9–9:17). The flood narrative is extremely complicated, raises difficult issues that go beyond the scope of this volume, and really deserves a book of its own. However, we will not ignore the flood totally because 6:1–8 gives the reason for God's frustration with humanity and 9:18–27 describes the beginning of humankind's new start after leaving the ark.

The stories I have chosen correspond to each other in using the special personal name for God, *Yahweh*. Most English translations, including the NRSV, render this name Yahweh as LORD written in capital and small capital letters (see 4:1; 4:26; 6:3; 9:26; 11:5). For about a hundred and fifty years now, biblical scholars have concluded that the first five books of the Old Testament originated as a compilation of various sources written at various times. The consistent use of *Yahweh* as God's name is one of many indications that the stories I have chosen were once part of a single, previously independent document. This hypothetical document, labeled the *Yahwist* and abbreviated as J, included other material in the books of Genesis, Exodus, and Numbers. Scholars theorize that the *Yahwist* was eventually incorporated along with other sources to form the Pentateuch, the first five books of the Hebrew Bible.

If you examine the texts from the first chapters of Genesis that I have *not* included in this book, you will see that they are associated with a special set of similar introductory formulas. In 2:4, the formula "These are the generations of the heavens and the earth," concludes 1:1–2:4 and simultaneously introduces what comes next. This same formula (translated in various ways in the NRSV) is used in 5:1; 10:1, and 11:10 to introduce genealogies, and in 6:9 to introduce the flood. Scholars attribute these formulas and the material associated with them to an author later than the Yahwist, known as the "Priestly Writer" or P. To sum up, I have set the flood aside and then chosen to discuss the stories from the Yahwist (J), while passing over material from the Priestly Writer (P).

"Did God Say...?" (Genesis 3:1)

This, of course, is the first question that Snake asks of Woman. Go back and review 2:16–17 and 3:1–5 slowly and carefully. In effect, Snake is asking: "What do God's words spoken in 2:16–17 really mean? Interpret them. Does what I am saying ('you shall not eat from *any* tree') correspond to what God actually said?" To respond, Woman must engage in the first episode of human interpretation.

We readers know that Woman did not hear God's prohibition directly in the story world of Genesis, for she was not fashioned until 2:22. We must assume that Man has conveyed it to her. Snake prompts Woman to interpret what she has heard that God said, in other words to read between the lines. Snake asks, in effect, "What do God's words 'mean' for you? Do God's words mean that you are to eat from no tree at all?" With his question, Snake introduces to Woman (and to us) the idea of a plurality of meanings and the ambiguity of words, even God's words.

In response, Woman restates God's prohibition in an interpreted, modified form. She adds "in the middle of the garden" and "nor shall you touch it" (3:2–3). These two changes indicate what God's words mean to her now, after she has engaged in some interpretation. In Woman's mind the tree of knowledge has become the central tree, "in the middle of the garden" from her perspective. Second, Woman indicates that it has become important for her to go beyond God's simple command not to eat. Because Snake has spotlighted the forbidden tree for her, she reinterprets God's words into to a more rigorous and absolute prohibition: "nor shall you touch it."

Snake then offers up some subversive truths, exaggerated truths, to suggest that important information has been withheld from Woman (3:4–5). "You will not die," Snake says, and they didn't, at least right away. "Your eyes will be opened," it promises, and they were. "God knows...you will be like God, knowing good and evil," it insinuates. What God says in 3:22 supports this. However, Snake uses these three partial truths in a deceptive manner, in the style of a modern political ad that combines literally true facts to communicate a misleading message. Crafty Snake has shifted the argument. Now the issue is no longer *what* God prohibited, but *why*—and what the actual consequences of eating would be. Snake incites Woman to ask herself, "What does God's command say about God's character and God's good will for my husband and me? Has God told us the complete truth?"

Snake's questions become a catalyst for Woman's quest to find meaning in God's words, for her act of interpretation, and eventually for her free choice to take and eat. She looks at the tree and "interprets" it (3:6). She is curious, open to alternatives. What does this tree "mean" from her perspective? Remember that she does not yet know "good and evil" or how to distinguish good from evil! So she perceives the tree as "good."

We readers know that some of what she sees is right on target. Like all the trees in the garden, this tree is "good for food and a delight to the eyes" (compare 2:9). It is true that having one's eyes opened is something like being made wise. However, in interpreting the tree, she also interprets God's command in a way that leads her to disobey it. She does not seem to judge the tree's value in the light of the command she has received. Her eyes are not yet opened to the potential for good and evil, so she naively fails to perceive that the "facts" that Snake has suggested may be more complicated than they appear to be on the surface.

As a result, based on her interpretation of God's command and of the tree's value, she takes its fruit and shares it with Man, who eats without further ado. The consequences that follow, both good and bad, have been triggered by the first human act of interpretation. This is a cautionary tale, perhaps, about the results of a bad choice based on a mistaken interpretation. However, Woman's choice is also the beginning of an exciting adventure for the human race. "The eyes of both were opened" (3:7). In some ways, of course, this was a bad thing. Yet many readers of Genesis over the centuries have suggested that their opened eyes and their new knowledge have turned out to be a good thing in the long run, or at least a mixed blessing. Woman and Man were enlightened as their eyes opened up and they gained new knowledge. Yet, opened eyes also meant the discovery of their nakedness and vulnerability, which led to fear, fig leaf aprons, and hiding in the trees (3:7–8, 10). Perhaps the most important result was that Woman and Man were now grown-ups. They would have to leave the "kindergarten of Eden" behind them and move out into the adult world.

This tale about the first human act of interpretation is a sobering lesson. For the most part, Man and Woman failed. Woman blames her failure on having listened to an outside voice: "The serpent tricked me" (3:13). She has reinterpreted her earlier interpretation! Reevaluating what has happened to her, she now judges that she was literally *mis*guided. Man's excuse is self-serving and superficial: "[Woman] gave me…" (3:12). God, however, understands this in the same way that Woman understands her error, namely as an interpretive failure caused by listening to another: "Because you have listened to the voice of your wife" (3:17).

As we follow Woman's primary act of interpretation, we find ourselves launched on our own interpretive adventure. We have questions, too. What then is the meaning of "in the day that you eat of it you shall die" in 2:17, restated by Woman in 3:3, and contradicted by Snake in 3:4? What are we to make of the fact that they continue to live? Is being "crafty" (3:1) a bad thing, or does it mean something more like prudent or clever? What does "knowledge of good and evil" actually mean? How are Man and Woman now "like God"?

"The Language of All the Earth" (Genesis 11:9)

One of the biggest challenges we face in interpreting the Old Testament is that it is written in Hebrew. Genesis has to be translated into English for most of us, and that creates a tricky distance between reader and story. Translators seek to reproduce the dynamic meaning of the Bible's original words in modern languages, but in doing this they must necessarily give up any hope of producing a word-for-word, literal translation.

Genesis itself knows about the vital importance of language for being truly human, but also examines the problems created among us by the fact of language differences. Man begins the structure of language when he starts naming animals with common nouns (2:19) and continues the process in formulating the words "Woman" and "Man" (2:23). Soon there are proper names too: Eve, Cain, the city Enoch, Shem, Enosh (3:20; 4:1, 17, 25, 26). As a result of all this inventiveness in language, humanity once had "one language" and "the same words" (11:1). The story of the tower-city of Babel begins by affirming that shared language can lead to fruitful cooperation without misunderstanding. Now in our post-Babel world, however, human cooperation and understanding have been complicated immeasurably by the confusion of language (11:7, 9).

The need to read the Bible in English means that our interpretations are easily muddled by the need for translation. For example, the word for "woman" and "wife" is the same in Hebrew (*ʾiššah*). The person who reads Genesis 2–3 in Hebrew experiences the same word for "woman" used seventeen times. However, in six of those occurrences, someone who reads from the NRSV will see instead the English word "wife" (2:24, 25; 3:8, 17, 20, 21). Reading in English means missing patterns and connections present in the original.

Here is a second example. As we shall see, the words for "ground" and "earth" appear throughout the Genesis stories from Eden to Babel. However, the interaction of languages means that the Hebrew word (*ʾereṣ*) most often translated as "earth" (that is, "the world on which we live"), has to be translated by NRSV as "land" (that is "country" or "territory") in 2:11, 12, 13; 4:16; 11:2. The word *ʾădāmah* is usually translated as "ground," but in 4:14 and 9:20 the NRSV translators have chosen to use "soil" instead. This all gets really strange when "earth" is used to translate its usual equivalent *ʾereṣ* in 6:4, 5, and 6, but is also used to translate *ʾădāmah* in 6:7 (for no good reason that I can see). However, *ʾădāmah* is rendered by its usual equivalent "ground" in 6:1! To help untangle this problem, a Hebrew word list at the front of this book lists places where the NRSV has obscured significant connections by translating identical Hebrew words with different English words. It must be emphasized, however, that these problems are not necessarily the fault of translators, whose task it is to produce a natural, fluent English text.

The huge number of available English translations further intensifies the impact of Babel for the interpreter. Each of these versions approaches the task of translation differently and ends up with different results. My experience as a Bible study leader convinces me that there is not much value in having several different translations on the table unless you have some idea why they are different. For this reason, and to make sure that I as author and you as reader stay "on the same page," I have chosen to use the NRSV as the foundation for our work together. The NRSV is a moderately literal translation produced by a body of highly respected scholars and based on the most recent advances in biblical research.

Step One: Bracket Off What You "Know"

One of the essential skills that a responsible interpreter needs to develop can be summarized in the challenge: *Bracket off what you think you already "know" about the text; read with an open mind* (see Step 1 in "Steps in Interpretation").

Most of us have ingrained presuppositions about what familiar Bible stories mean. This is especially true with regard to old favorites such as Adam and Eve or Cain and Abel. However, experienced interpreters learn to put those prejudgments "on the shelf" when they first approach a text, no matter how often they may have encountered it in the past. This process of ignoring or temporarily forgetting tried-and-true traditional meanings is sometimes called "bracketing." Imagine putting brackets or parentheses around what you think you know about the snake in Eden or the tower in Babel so that you can read a familiar text with unbiased, new eyes.

The discipline of bracketing is especially important for the opening stories of Genesis because traditional views of what they mean are so deep-seated in the Christian mindset. Everybody knows that Eve was created to be Adam's subordinate assistant and "helpmate." Everybody knows that the Eden story is about the first sin and the fall of humanity from an original perfect state into ongoing imperfection and original sin. Tempted by Satan, Eve fell into sin and dragged Adam down with her. Everybody knows that humanity was originally intended to be immortal, but that God punished us with death because of that first sin. Everybody knows that this sin was continued and intensified by Cain's heartless murder of his brother, and that Cain was punished with a distinctive mark. Everybody knows that God cursed Noah's son Ham and all his descendants. Everybody knows that the tower in Babel was built to threaten God's realm in heaven and that God stopped its construction to protect heaven from humanity's assault.

However, when one actually starts to read these stories with care and an independent mind, much of what "everybody knows" turns out to be just plain false or certainly open to more than one interpretation. Although you can find it in the dictionary, "helpmate" is really a misunderstanding and corruption of the *King James Version's* rendering "help meet for him" (in modern English, "co-worker appropriate for him"; NRSV "helper as his partner"). If you look carefully, you will see that neither sin nor Satan is ever mentioned in the Eden story. Snake was only identified with Satan much later (in the Apocrypha, for example, Wisdom of Solomon 2:24), and this post-Old Testament connection is only hinted at in Revelation 12:9 and 20:2. Sin is not mentioned until the story of Cain. Genesis 4:15 makes it clear that Cain's mark was given by God to protect him, not to punish him. God doesn't curse Ham. Instead, it is Noah who speaks the curse, and it is only directed against Ham's son Canaan, not all the descendants of Ham (9:24–25). There is no hint that God feels threatened by what the Babel builders are up to in 11:1–9, and the tower doesn't seem to be the most important element in their construction project anyway.

Some traditionally accepted interpretations seem to be just plain dangerous. As we have already pointed out, 9:18–27 says absolutely nothing about a curse on Noah's son Ham. Yet even though Ham was supposedly the ancestor of peoples in Palestine and Arabia as well as Africa (10:6–7), many white Christians in the period before the Civil War found justification in Noah's curse to support the institution of slavery. Many thoughtful Christians believe it is hazardous to use Genesis 2–11 as a science textbook from which to draw information about the origins of the human race or the geological effects of a worldwide flood. Certainly most teachers of science on the high school and college level believe it is intellectually dangerous to teach students religious views side-by-side, or even in place of, scientific truth about these matters.

A more delicate problem has to do with the way later interpreters, including some New Testament authors, have understood Woman's role in the story of Eden. In 1 Corinthians 11:7–10, a passage universally acknowledged as extremely difficult to understand, Paul argues that when women pray or prophesy in church they must not do so with their heads uncovered, a practice that may have been culturally linked to licentious behavior. In part, Paul argues on the basis of the sequence in which the first two humans were created, Man first and Woman only second. However, it is important to note that Paul also goes on to insist that the sexes are interdependent and interrelated "in the Lord" (vv. 11–12). A similar argument from creation sequence is advanced in 1 Timothy 2:13 in the context of a paragraph urging that contemporary cultural norms be followed and that women not exercise teaching authority over men (1 Tim. 2:8–15). The situation seems to have been that certain teachers, including women, were advocating that Christian women follow a celibate lifestyle. To counter this problem and to lend support to his organizational guideline that women not teach, the author of 1 Timothy points out that it was Eve who was deceived and sinned, in contrast to Adam who was not deceived. This particular way of reading the temptation story also appears in the Apocrypha in Sirach 25:24. My point here is not to argue for or against the imposition of these ancient cultural norms about women's roles on modern church practice. Rather, I am urging that as a responsible interpreter you should bracket off all such prejudgments about meaning and hold them in abeyance until you have had a chance to interact with the stories of Genesis on your own.

After all, the Genesis text itself draws no conclusions about the respective status of Man and Woman until the "curse scene" (3:16), in which Woman's status as one ruled over by her husband is presented as a consequence of eating the forbidden fruit, not something implicit in the sequence of creation. In fact, God makes it clear that things are "not good" with the initial male-only situation (2:18). Creation only reaches a proper state of affairs when God builds Woman out of Man to act as his partner. Then Man greets her as a wonderful addition to the scheme of things ("at last"!) and as a person corresponding to himself as his very bone and flesh (2:23). It seems to me pretty hard to derive male superiority out of this presentation. In fact, some early rabbinical interpreters suggested that Woman was created second as a somewhat improved version of Man. Other rabbis pointed out that being first in creation does not necessarily imply superiority—after all, in Genesis 1 God created gnats before humans!

As far as Woman being deceived goes, the story apparently indicates that Man was actually present during Woman's conversation with Snake ("with her," 3:6). Certainly, Woman was tricked, but at least she thought about things and considered her options. Man just ate what he was given (3:6, 12).

Having said this, however, we cannot deny that Genesis 2–3 shares with the rest of the Old Testament a negative and patriarchal attitude toward women. The Eden story is told from the male point of view. God creates humanity by creating Man. This first Man is a male human being from the beginning, although he only later discovers himself to be male when he is confronted by Woman (2:23). God prohibits Man, not Man and Woman, from eating from the tree. God eventually creates Woman, but this is done to meet a lack or insufficiency in Man's existence. Woman is taken from Man, who is primary and already exists. Her name "Woman" is (supposedly) derived from the simpler and more fundamental word "man" as male (2:23). Only Man's reaction is described when God presents the two lovebirds to each other. In Genesis 3:17–19, 22–24, Woman's explicit presence disappears from the story. It seems clear, then, that the author is primarily concerned with Man as the representative of humanity and only includes Woman when her presence is required for the story to work.

Experience has taught me that people usually find evidence in Scripture to support whatever it is that they already believe, or want to believe, or feel most comfortable believing. Luther often remarked that interpreters shape and twist the Bible to suit their own fancy "as if it were a wax nose to be pulled to and fro" ("On the Papacy in Rome against the Most Celebrated Romanist in Leipzig," *Luther's Works,* vol. 39 [Philadelphia: Fortress Press, 1970], 81). This is inevitable, but we can at least limit our natural human tendencies by bracketing off our presumptions and presuppositions and by paying disciplined attention to the words actually on the page before us, not the words we wish were there or always thought were there.

Fall and Original Sin

Sometimes the presuppositions the interpreter should bracket off originate from the way that other parts of the Bible have understood these stories and from the interpretations of influential early theologians. An example of this is the commonly accepted notion that sin and death were first introduced into human existence when Man and Woman ate the fruit. According to this viewpoint, Genesis 3 describes the "fall of humanity" understood as a completely negative episode with no positive consequences. In *Paradise Lost,* John Milton famously describes the time-honored view that the Eden story tells

> Of man's first disobedience, and the fruit
> Of that forbidden tree, whose mortal taste
> Brought death into the world, and all our woe.

As I have already noted, however, the word for "sin" does not occur in the Eden story and does not make its first explicit appearance until the description of Cain's moral struggle in Genesis 4:7. Nor does the Eden story, taken by itself, ever claim that humanity was originally intended to be immortal. All the reader can say for certain is that the story concludes with God making sure that immortality would be unavailable to us (3:22–24) and that the natural and expected consequence of our having been formed from dust would be the result (3:19).

The Old Testament itself never alludes to the Eden story in terms of a fall of humanity into universal sin and death. This is not even done by Job's friends, for whom it would have made a perfect argument to undermine his protestations of complete innocence. It is only in Jewish literature later than the Hebrew Bible that the idea of a fall is proclaimed (Wisdom of Solomon 2:24; 2 Esdras 3:4–7, 21–22, 26, in the Apocrypha). Saint Paul followed this lead and interpreted Eden in terms of a fall into death and sin, most notably in Romans 5:12–17.

I am not suggesting that there is anything wrong with Paul's interpretation or that the Christian church ought to abandon the concept of original sin or inborn human sinfulness. My point is rather that there are other legitimate (and perhaps even more convincing) ways of reading the garden of Eden story. These alternative readings should not be obscured or short-circuited by a rush to interpretive judgment. To see clearly everything that is being said in Genesis 2–3, we are going to have to set Paul aside for the time being.

The notion of original sin, that all human beings are trapped at birth into inevitable sinfulness, was bequeathed to Christian doctrine by the early theologian Augustine, although it is certainly implied in Paul (Rom. 3:23; 5:19; 8:19–23). It is instructive, however, to discover that some church fathers before Augustine read the Eden story the other way around. Those ancient Christian thinkers saw Genesis 2–3 as biblical evidence that human beings are *not* inexorably bound by the dictates of impersonal fate, but instead have free will in choosing what they choose (compare Sirach 15:11–20 in the Apocrypha). The ancient Greeks and Romans tended to assume that the inscrutable forces of destiny compelled people to make certain choices. In contrast, the Eden story indicates that the first human pair made their choice to eat the fruit based completely on free will. They may have been tempted or tricked, but no uncontrollable force compelled them to violate God's prohibition. In connection with this, interpreters before Augustine often used this story to teach behavioral lessons: avoid gluttony, marry only once, remain celibate. In other words, although reading the Eden story as describing a fall into entrapping sin and punitive death has been the traditional and "obvious" interpretation for many centuries now, such a reading was not always seen as the only possible or reasonable one.

Step Ten: Eden in Context

Attention to context is vital in biblical interpretation. Accordingly, Step 10 of the "Steps in Interpretation" is, *How does context shape how you read the text, and how does the text contribute to its own context?*

For example, how are we to understand Genesis 2−3 in light of Genesis 1? Biblical scholarship indicates that different authors wrote these two versions of creation at different times for different sets of readers. However, now these two creation stories stand next to each other so that they cannot be read in isolation. One way to conceive of the relationship between Genesis 1 and Genesis 2−3 is to consider the Eden story as a flashback to what has already been recounted in 1:24−30. That is to say, Genesis 2−3 goes back to replay in greater detail one episode in Genesis 1, doing so from a perspective more oriented to human relationships and development. Alternatively, one might think in terms of photography. Genesis 1 uses a wide-angle lens to portray a general panorama. The next two chapters "zoom in" to examine specific details.

The story of Eden points forward to subsequent narratives. The four rivers of 2:10−14 show that Genesis 2−3 has implications beyond what took place within the limits of Eden. This paragraph points outward from Eden to the world of nations that become the topic of other stories in Genesis. Likewise, God's address to unnamed other beings ("like us") in 3:22 takes us beyond earthly limits to heavenly matters, a concern that will reappear in Genesis 6:1−4 and 11:7.

Other ties between the Eden story and upcoming narratives include:

- The question, "What is this that you have done/What have you done?" directed to Woman in 3:13 and Cain in 4:10
- The interplay between desire and mastery in regard to Woman and her husband (3:16) and Cain and sin (4:7)
- The theme of agricultural labor (2:5, 15; 3:17, 23; 4:3; 9:20)
- God taking an action in order to see (2:19 and 11:5)
- Seeing that something is good (3:6 and 6:1, where "good" is translated "fair")
- Nakedness and knowing (3:7 and 9:23−24)

The theme that humans make bad decisions that have a potential to do great harm will reappear in the stories of Cain (4:1−16), the prelude to the flood (6:1−8), and Babel (11:1−9). Dangerous human potential will again need to be controlled, by a mark on Cain, by limits on human life span, and by language confusion.

   Commentators have often traced a plot of ever-increasing sin in these tales, a sort of snowball effect from Eden to Cain to Noah to Babel. I think this commonly accepted notion is difficult to maintain. Certainly each of these stories has as its catalyst an incident of crime or impropriety: eating, murder, readiness for vengeance, boundary-breaking sex, drunkenness and disrespect, building a city and tower. Certainly, these early humans are presented as having a propensity to misbehave, although as already mentioned, the word for "sin" is used only once (4:7). However, there is really no increase in human wickedness. The low point of individual transgression seems to be reached with Cain's murder, and humanity as a whole seems to be most wicked just before the flood (6:5–8). Trespass continues after the flood, individually with Ham and communally with the citizens of Babel, but there does not seem to be any increase in its intensity or seriousness.

   In fact, if we are willing to bracket off preconceived ideas, we discover disconcerting elements of ambiguity in each of these episodes. In the story of Adam and Eve, we wonder: What *is* the knowledge of good and evil? What is so bad about having it? Why would having one's eyes opened be a problem? Don't Man and Woman achieve much (insight, maturity) as well as lose much? Moreover, the actual motivations of the first pair remain ambiguous and unspecified. There seems to be no direct link between Snake's words (3:1, 4–5) and Eve's subsequent thoughts (3:6).

   Moving to the other stories, Cain's deed is unambiguously wrong, an act of murder and sin, but the story itself unfolds into an explanation for God's imposition of limits on human vengeance. The nature and implications of Lamech's speech later in Genesis 4 are obscure, not explicit. In 6:1–4, humans do not commit the offense; rather it is the "sons of God" who violate the proper order of things. The universal human propensity for wickedness in 6:5–8 is never really illustrated or specified. The consequences of Ham's offense against his father Noah (9:21–22) are deflected onto Ham's son Canaan in an odd way. In the Babel story, we are never really told what is wrong with building this impressive city with its lofty tower. The text never mentions human arrogance. To say the tower's top was "in the heavens" indicates that it was really tall, but implies nothing about a human assault on divine prerogatives. What then is wrong with the builders' desire to acquire a name and their disinclination to be scattered?

   The stories in Genesis 2–11 share several common themes. Knowledge and nakedness are stressed in the Eden story and reappear in the story of Noah and Ham (2:25; 3:7, 10, 11; 9:22–24). The topic of revenge holds the two parts of Genesis 4 together. As we shall see, an ongoing correspondence and interaction between human and ground hold together Genesis 2–4; 6:1–8; 9:18–27; and 11:1–9.

Another common theme is multiplication, the growth from few to many. The narrative focus moves from an individual (2:7) to a couple (2:22–23) to a family (4:1–2). Genealogies for Cain in 4:17–24 and Seth in 4:25–26 suggest population expansion. Population growth is made explicit in 6:1 and in the post-flood peopling of the earth (9:18–19). Finally, humanity moves from being a single people located in one place to unfold into a multitude of ethnic groups (11:6–9).

Dispersal provides another continuing theme. The stories begin with the humans in one place, in Eden in the east (2:8, 15). However, they are driven away from there, and guardian cherubim are stationed to the east of the garden to prevent their return (3:22–24). Likewise, Cain becomes a wanderer, driven away from the ground (4:12–13), and settles "east of Eden" (4:16). In Genesis 11, humanity moves "from the east" (11:2) and settles in one city, hoping to avoid being dispersed over the earth (11:4). But in the end Yahweh scatters them far and wide (11:8–9).

How Scripture Works

Part of the difficulty we have in being open to new interpretations lies in the commonly accepted notion that every verse and paragraph of the Bible has only *one* correct meaning or interpretation. We have been conditioned to think that if Eden describes the fall of humanity into original sin and death, then it cannot mean anything else. This simplistic, one-dimensional point of view is implicit in a question like "What is *the* meaning of this passage?" as though only one meaning can be present or permitted. This treats the Bible as a source book of objectively true propositions, rather than as a rich and flexible collection of stories, poems, laws, letters, and histories gathered over the course of a thousand years. In my view, the Bible becomes a living book, a living Word, only when it is read, interpreted, and communicated by and among God's people. When this happens, God's Holy Spirit uses Scripture as an instrument or a means to communicate God's Word. This is what Luther meant when he said of the Bible, "Here you will find the swaddling cloth and the manger in which Christ lies" ("Preface to the Old Testament," *Luther's Works*, vol. 35 [Philadelphia: Muhlenberg Press, 1960], 236).

In contrast to this desire to achieve a single correct interpretation, Jewish interpreters accept multiple interpretations. The many diverse opinions of past readers all stand together as part of the treasure of Jewish interpretive tradition. Rabbis were willing to ask an enormously wide range of questions about biblical texts. One classic example is, "What part of Adam was Eve made from: his rib, his tail, his face, or his side?" This question is possible because the Hebrew word usually translated as "rib" (2:21–22) can be taken to mean something like "side," as of a hill or a building.

To engage in the adventure of self-directed reading and self-reliant interpretation, one needs a dynamic and flexible view of how Scripture works. Let me describe how I approach this issue.

My first point is that Scripture literally *works*. The Bible is not an inactive sourcebook in which information about God or about ethics remains passively stored until we access it. The Bible's own testimony about itself is that God's Word is active and produces results (Isa. 55:10–11; Jer. 23:29; 2 Tim. 3:16–17; Heb. 4:12–13). These passages indicate that Scripture works as an active agent for change. It transforms individuals and communities. It generates apprehension and forms faith. It warns us, urges us to action, encourages us, and reorients our priorities. The Bible is not so much a religious encyclopedia or a source of eternal truths set forth in proof texts as it is an effective tool used by God to get under our skin and create anxiety, faith, and action.

Second, understanding the Bible in this manner helps us think about the inspiration of Scripture in dynamic rather than static ways. People often limit the location of divine inspiration to the work of the original writers (the "men and women moved by the Holy Spirit" of 2 Pet. 1:20) and within the words of the biblical text itself (compare Heb. 3:7: "the Holy Spirit says"). However, I believe it is also useful to think of inspiration as a "live-action," contemporary event that takes place when we read and hear the Bible. God's Spirit inspires the Bible in the here and now as the Bible interacts dynamically with its readers to do the work God wants it to do—to transform, create faith, warn, motivate, encourage, reorient. Understood in this sense, the Bible becomes God's Word as it acts on those who read it.

The third point is a difficult one, and I ask for your patience before you reject it out of hand. In the Old Testament, truth is often set forth in material that librarians would label "fiction" rather than "nonfiction." Sometimes the Old Testament presents its theology in the form of poetry (as in the book of Psalms), sometimes as proverbs, sometimes as history or laws. But quite often, in a way similar to Jesus' use of parables, Old Testament Scripture uses narrative or storytelling as a channel to communicate theological truth. This is especially true in the early chapters of Genesis, in which the authors retell popular folktales to express Israel's beliefs about God and what God expected from them.

Fourth, as I have already claimed, texts have more than one "right" meaning. Paul insists that the stories in Genesis about Abraham demonstrate Abraham's faith (Rom. 4; Gal. 3:6–18). Yet James insists that those same stories serve to illustrate the importance of good works as something essential to faith (Jas. 2:21–23). Both interpretations are certainly right. Likewise Rahab, a character in the book of Joshua, serves as a symbol of faithful works in James 2:25, but of active faith in Hebrews 11:31. Ephesians 5:25–32 applies Genesis 2:23–24 to the mystery of Christ and the church. In Mark 10:6–9, Jesus reads this same text as a witness to the permanence of marriage. Yet again, Paul in 1 Corinthians 6:15–16 uses this very same text to prohibit sexual immorality. These examples show that the meanings of scriptural texts are open, not closed. As we dig more deeply into these Genesis stories, we will discover a multitude of uncertainties, puns, loose connections, ambiguous words and phrases—all open to a variety of interpretations. Church history demonstrates that there can be no one right interpretation for every reader in every age.

Finally, the stories of the Bible reflect realities about the people who read them. A person's reading of the Eden story will likely reveal something about his or her mind-set concerning relationships between women and men. Our deep-seated feelings about sexuality, human self-sufficiency, and free will will be reflected back at us when we read about Adam and Eve, Snake, and the tree of knowledge. Our attitude about urban life will affect how we understand the cities described in Genesis 4:17 or 11:1–9 and whether we see the tower of Babel as an example of human arrogance or an expected part of a city skyline. We may recognize our own prejudicial attitudes in the ethnic insults directed against Canaanites (9:25–27) and Babylonians (11:9). Americans can hardly read about the slavery imposed on Ham's son Canaan without feeling uneasy.

Modern readers are often conscious of features that failed to interest Christians of earlier ages. For example, previous readers of Genesis typically focused only on the creation and punishment of humanity. However, ecologically sensitive modern readers tend to notice that the earth is also an important focus. We read that the earth brings forth plants (2:5–6; 3:23) and that animals are related to humanity (2:19; 3:15). We discover disharmony in humanity's relationship with the earth and the negative effects that human violence can have on nature (3:17–18; 4:11–12). While we are reading the Bible, it turns out that the Bible is also reading us, revealing to us truths about ourselves, often uncomfortable truths.

Biblical texts are dynamic. They have an effect on those who read them. They were written down and gathered into the Bible to make a difference in people's lives. Biblical texts instruct us. Sometimes they work to change the status quo or move against an attitude the reader may have. Sometimes they urge the reader to take action. Sometimes they seem to be intended to change our attitudes, encourage us, or inspire us. They may condemn us, urge us to repent, or strengthen our faith. They may comfort us or disturb us. Readers may be forced to reorient their priorities. The dynamic nature of Scripture is addressed by the question: *What is the text's purpose or intention or goal? What is it designed to do to you as reader; how does it affect or change you?* (Step 9 in "Steps in Interpretation").

Discipline

The skills of self-reliant interpretation take time and effort to acquire. As is the case with any craft or trade, there are disciplines to learn and practice.

- Practice "close reading."
- Read the text slowly and carefully several times through, and write down points and questions that occur to you.
- Allow for multiple meanings.
- Check your conclusions and thoughts by carefully focusing on the words that are actually on the page before you.
- Avoid speculating on the motives of the characters or their inner thoughts, unless the text gives you a reason to do so.
- Be willing to accept that some questions you have cannot be answered.

We have already touched on "close reading," reading slowly and carefully and writing down notes, allowing multiple meanings, and focusing on the words actually on the page. Two other disciplines are important.

First, avoid speculating on the motives of the characters or their inner thoughts unless the text gives you a reason to do so. Modern authors usually give readers a window on the emotions and motivations of characters. We are used to being told how someone is feeling and why they are behaving in a certain way. The authors of the Bible rarely do this, so we are tempted to fill in the blanks. Snake must have been an enemy of God, we think, but the text never reveals its motives. We imagine that Man and Woman must have felt embarrassed by their nakedness, but the text only speaks of fear. Is God feeling angry or sorrowful when Man and Woman are driven from Eden? The words on the page tell us nothing about God's emotions. Sometimes we are given this sort of information about characters (see 4:5; 6:6–7), but usually not. Skilled interpreters avoid making unwarranted assumptions about emotions and motivations. Second, be willing to accept that some questions you have cannot be answered. Generations of readers have wondered about things like where Cain's wife came from (4:17) or why God failed to acknowledge Cain's sacrifice (4:5) or why Noah curses his innocent grandson Canaan instead of his guilty son Ham (9:25). Many answers have been suggested over the years, but none have been widely accepted. The truth is that we may desperately want to know something but may never get a satisfactory answer. Practiced interpreters know when to give up and move on.

Sources

My "eyes were opened" to seeing Woman's encounter with the tree as an act of thoughtful interpretation by Phyllis Trible, *God and the Rhetoric of Sexuality* (Philadelphia: Fortress Press, 1978), 108–13. Beverly J. Stratton, *Out of Eden: Reading, Rhetoric, and Ideology in Genesis 2–3,* JSOTSup 208 (Sheffield: Sheffield Academic Press, 1995), 86–91, also stimulated my thinking. On Augustine and the other church fathers, see Elaine Pagels, *Adam, Eve, and the Serpent* (New York: Random House, 1988).

Several Bible translations are more literal than NRSV and seek to come closer to a word-for-word correspondence with the original languages. Using the older *Revised Standard Version* (1952) side by side with the NRSV is a practical way of discovering patterns and correspondences that the NRSV has obscured. The *New American Standard Bible* (revised 1995) is probably the most literal modern version. The *English Standard Version* (2001) is a revision of the RSV and another literal translation.

CHAPTER 2

Babes in the Wood
Genesis 2–3

In the Introduction, I outlined the interpretive method we will be using (see "Steps in Interpretation"). I am counting on you to do each step on your own before moving on to read my thoughts. In chapter 1, I touched on the steps involving "bracketing off," context, and purpose. In this chapter, we will take up several other steps, beginning with the second one: *What is familiar about the text? How are we like the first readers?* Spend some time applying this question to Genesis 2:4–3:24. Do your work with a pencil or pen in hand, and write down your ideas. Keep at it until you come up with some sort of result for each step. Compare your results with my thoughts.

Step Two: What Is Familiar?

We know that gardens are watered and need to be tilled and kept lest they grow wild. We know the fatal attraction of "forbidden fruit." We are familiar with the marriage patterns of 2:24 and the history of male domination reflected in 3:16. Many of us find snakes intimidating and have an urge to destroy them (3:15). Childbearing is painful, yet women do not seek to avoid it. Work is frustrating, and farming is a precarious way to earn a living (3:17–18). Returning to dust may seem to be a relief after a lifetime of toil (note the "until" in 3:19).

25

Eden is a familiar world in many ways. Actions have consequences. Sexuality is foundational to human life and warmly affirmed (2:23). At the same time, as is also the case in our world, Eden houses ambiguity—prohibitions without explanation, options available for choice, the presentation of different perspectives. God is one determinative element in human life, but by no means the only one. Indeed, God has complicated human life by making attractive trees and a crafty snake.

These first humans are familiar characters. They share our capacities for language, organization, vocation, and sexual attraction. Woman (at least) is willing to ask questions and entertain new perceptions (3:2–6). She questions authority. Like us, she takes aesthetic pleasure in what is good to eat and pretty to look at. Like us, these two humans are open to verbal deception (Woman) and peer pressure (Man). We, too, make decisions based on free will; and quite often these decisions turn out to be bad ones. We understand feelings of shame and fear (3:7–10). We, too, take inadequate measures to cope with these feelings and have our own psychological equivalents of fig leaves and hiding behind trees. Conceivably, we might also take a little human pride in the resiliency of our first ancestors! Even after curse and expulsion, these two tough humans carry on. Man names Woman "Mother" (3:20), and they persevere in producing a new generation (4:1–2, 25).

One enduring connection between the story told in Genesis 2–3 and our world is its emphasis on *etiology*, that is, the urge to discover the original causes that lie behind our present situation. Etiology seeks to answer the universal yearning to know how things got started and why things are the way they are. These are the sorts of questions children love to ask, and elements in Genesis 2–3 seem to be designed to respond to a child's eternal "Why?" The contours of marriage and the life of agriculture outside of Eden are both introduced by an etiological "therefore" (2:24; 3:23). The four rivers flowing out to the four corners of the world explain global geography as the ancients would have pictured it (2:10–14). A repeated pattern of "once there was none but now there is" works to explain the present. Once upon a time there was *no* plant, herb, or man to till the ground (2:5), but these realities come into existence by the time the story is over (3:18, 23). The lonely existence of a single human individual was "*not* good," so animals emerge (2:18–19). A helper was "*not* found," so God made Woman (2:20–21).

The Eden story explains our world. How did earth become fertile and productive? Why are women and men sexually attracted to each other? Why is humanity at war with snakes? Where did agricultural life and our diet based on it come from? How did clothing originate? Why are we buried in the ground and decompose back into it?

At a deeper level, the story also explores more philosophical issues. What does it mean to be human, to be a man or a woman? Why is sex so delightful, problematic, and powerful? Why is language so potent and enigmatic? (Think of Snake's questions.) How do we make choices? (Think of Woman's response.) What is the relationship between perception and reality? (How can you be naked and not know it? Did Woman perceive the tree correctly?) Why is life so hard, and why does it end in dusty death? Why are humans and God so similar in important ways and yet so different when it comes to immortality?

Perhaps the most basic question that Eden seeks to resolve concerns what has gone wrong with human existence. Why are we engaged in constant conflict—Woman versus Man, human versus animal, mortal versus God? Why are we overworked? Why do we bear children in pain? Eden is not really a story about the origin of sin and moral evil (see chapter 1), but about what happened when humans started to make independent judgments about what was good and autonomous choices based on those judgments. The result was a loss of childlike innocence. Humanity's eyes were opened to perceive the harsh realities that surrounded them. Nor is it quite correct to say that the story explains how death entered the world. Instead, it describes how human immortality was prevented.

Step Three: What Is Unfamiliar?

Now ask this question of the Eden story: *What is unfamiliar? What surprises, puzzles, or shocks you? How are we different from the first readers?* No cheating! Try to answer this question on your own before moving on. Write down some notes on your thoughts.

Eden is not the ordinary world we live in. Some of our feelings of distance stem from cultural differences between the original readers and us. The rivers and nations described in 2:10–14 are mostly unknown to us, with the exception of the Tigris and Euphrates in present-day Iraq. We may wonder to whom God is addressing the "like us" of 3:22. However, the text's first readers would have understood without being told that God is talking to the divine beings or "junior-grade gods" who were thought to make up God's advisory council (see Gen. 1:26; 11:7 Ps. 82:1, 6–7; Isa. 6:8). The modern reader probably does not know that cherubim (3:24) were mythological winged beings and that statues of them were installed to serve as guardians for temples and palaces.

Other matters may surprise us because they seem to fit more into the realm of folktales than sober, realistic reporting. Such folkloristic elements include Woman's "backwards birth," a talking snake, and human conversations with God strolling about in an earthly garden. If we have previously read Genesis 1, we may be surprised to find that the order of creation in Genesis 2 is not animals first, then human beings as male and female together (as in 1:24–27) but instead Man first, then animals, then Woman.

Unlike us, ancient Israelite readers would have been familiar with other tales similar to Genesis 2–3, both from their own culture and from contact with other peoples. The prophet Ezekiel utilized facets of Israel's own folklore about First Man and a primeval fertile garden. He applied these story elements to the king of Tyre in Ezekiel 28:11–19 and used others to describe the future Jerusalem temple in Ezekiel 47:1–12. The Bible uses the garden of Eden (or of God) as a metaphor several times (Gen. 13:10; Isa. 51:3; Ezek. 31:8; 36:35; Joel 2:3), demonstrating that it was a well-known theme in Israel's culture. The Babylonians also preserved stories, sometimes surprisingly similar to those told in Israel, about the creation of humans by the gods and the complications that resulted *(Enuma Elish, Atrahasis),* and even about a plant that offered immortality but was stolen by a snake *(Gilgamesh).* Another difference between the first readers and many of us is that they would have been quite used to the notion that God expects people to abstain from certain foods (for example, Gen. 9:4; Ex. 22:31; Lev. 19:26).

Man and Woman in Eden seem to be rather peculiar people. It is as though they haven't grown up yet. Man is still developing his language skills (2:19–20, 23). Like very young children, they are not disturbed about being naked. They cannot yet tell the difference between things that are good and helpful and things that are bad and harmful (2:17; 3:5). They do not yet face a life of troublesome pregnancies and frustrating labor (3:16–19). In their innocence, they seem to be "babes in the wood."

Step Four: Key Words

What are the key words—words that are repeated or pivotal to the text's movement and meaning? A good way to discover key words is to run Genesis 2–3 through a photocopier. Then mark up the copy as you work and make lists.

You will have found some words that are used numerous times: *earth, eat, garden, good* (including the phrase "good and evil"), *ground, man, name* (as a verb and noun), *said, tree, woman. Man* and *woman,* and *good* and *evil,* are contrasting pairs and so will be considered in a subsequent section. Other words are used less often but are clearly important: *animal, command, cursed, day, dust, eyes, form, fruit, give, know* (and *knowledge*), *life* (*living, live*), *naked, see, take, till.*

How Key Words Work

Even if a word or phrase is only used twice, it can still be crucial to highlight transitions and changes. For example, *plant of the field* is something that does not exist as the story opens (2:5), but then becomes part of human reality as the story draws to its conclusion (3:18). The stream going up from the earth *watered* the ground (2:6), but when Eden is planted, a river flows out of it *to water* the garden (2:10). The repeated *brought...to the man* in 2:19 and 2:22 holds together the quest for a *helper as his partner* (2:18, 20) and highlights Man's subsequent act of naming Woman. The author has created a balance between the description of disobedience in 3:6: "*gave...to* her *husband* (= her *man*), who was *with her,* and *he ate*" and Man's defense in 3:12: "*the woman* whom you *gave* to be *with me, she gave...*and *I ate.*" *Cursed* and *eat all the days of your life* connect the penalties for Snake and human (3:14, 17). This connection is backed up by a repetition of *dust* in 3:14 and 19.

Your list of key words will probably not be perfect because you are using a translation. You can tell that animals are important to the story—as potential helpers named by Man and in the character of Snake. However, unless you read Hebrew you will not be able to see that two different expressions are used for animals. One word is translated *cattle* in 2:20 and *animals* in 3:14, while a different expression is rendered *animal of the field* in 2:19 and 20, but *wild animal* and *wild creature* in 3:1 and 3:14. Again, you would have to rely on an outside source such as a commentary to realize that *nostrils* in 2:7 and *face* in 3:19 are the same word and thus see the link provided between the initial creation of humanity and its final circumstances outside Eden. While using this book, at least, you can rely on the "Hebrew Word List" on pages vii–xii to help you with these issues of verbal equivalency.

Other hidden verbal identities in Genesis 2—3 are:

- *keep* in 2:15 and *guard* in 3:24
- *living being* for the human in 2:7 and *living creature* for the animals in 2:19

- *sound* in 3:8, 10 and *voice* in 3:17
- *midst* in 2:9, *middle* in 3:3, and *among* in 3:8
- *pangs* of Woman's childbearing in 3:16 and the *toil* of human agriculture in 3:17
- *reach out* in 3:22 and *sent forth* in 3:23

Sometimes key words help the reader see fine points in the narrative. For example, the concrete and "meaty" word *flesh* closes up the place where Man lost his rib (2:21) and also expresses the relational unity of man and woman: *my flesh* (2:23) and *one flesh* (2:24). *Fruit* seems to spotlight the desirability of the forbidden tree in that this word is only used in regard to the tree when Woman is talking about it or plucking it (3:2–3, 6), but not before or after, even when we might expect it (2:16–17; 3:11, 17). Similarly, the repeated use of *eyes* links the allure of the tree and the consequences of eating from it (3:5, 6, 7). A threefold repetition of *command* to designate the forbidden tree nicely encompasses prohibition (2:16), discovery (3:11), and consequences (3:17). Repetition of the phrase *the man and his wife* draws attention to the issue of nakedness and its consequences (2:25; 3:8, 21). *East* creates an envelope or frame around the whole story, locating Eden at the beginning and the roadblock back to it at the end (2:8; 3:24).

Repeated use of *all* and *every* (the same word in Hebrew) indicates that this story has universal significance. Universality characterizes life in primeval Eden: *every tree* and *any tree* in 2:9, 16; 3:1; *every animal* or *all cattle* or *any animal* in 2:19, 20; 3:1. The story of humanity and the world after Eden is also a universal one: *all animals* and *all wild creatures* in 3:14; *all the days of your life* in 3:14, 17; *mother of all living* in 3:20.

Life is obviously an important theme. The first human is endowed with the breath of *life* to become a *living* being like the animals (2:7, 19), fails to gain access to the immortality offered by the tree of *life* (2:9; 3:22, 24), and names Woman "mother of all *living*" (3:20).

The key words *man/human* (*ʾādām*) and *ground* (*ʾădāmah*) are related through a pun or play on words. You can see how it works by looking at the NRSV textual note for 2:7: *ʾādām* was taken from the *ʾădāmah*. *Ground* means land that can be cultivated, arable soil. Some translators have tried to capture this pun in English as "human from the humus" or "earthling from the earth." If you look at the occurrences of *ground* in the text, you can see how the relationship between *ground* and *man/human* stands at the very center of the story. At the beginning,

the *ground* cannot produce because there is no *man/human* to *till* it
(2:5; NRSV translates as "no one"). Near the end of the story, this
predicament has been taken care of. Having been driven from Eden,
the *man/human* is now available to "*till* the *ground*" (3:22–23). Thus
the story moves full circle from 2:6 to 3:23. All other relationships
line up around the association between *man/human* and *ground*. God
forms the first human from the ground (2:7). The trees of the garden
spring up from the ground (2:9). The animals too, are formed from
the ground (2:19), including Snake. Humans now spend their lives
tilling the ground (3:17, 23) and in the end return to the ground at
death (3:19).

Genesis 2:5–8: Form, Dust, Till, Garden

The verb *form* (2:7, 19) portrays a "hands-on" creation. God molds
the earthy material of dust the way a potter shapes clay. The same
language is used for God's forming of the animals, indicating the solid
relationship between humans and the animal kingdom. But the kinship
of having been "formed out of the ground" is not sufficiently close to
produce a "helper as...partner." Achieving this closer relationship
requires the more intimate action of taking out a rib (Hebrew:
"something off to the side") and making (literally "building") Woman
around it. This operation is so radical that God must repair the resulting
cavity with more tissue. Only this sort of radical surgery was able to
create a "bone and flesh" relationship.

God shapes earthy *dust* as raw material (2:7). *Dust* implies that
limitations are set on human existence even at the very start of the
story. This limitation is eventually confirmed by Snake's lowly fate
(3:14) and in the present-day reality of 3:19. Snake eats *dust* like a
defeated enemy (Ps. 72:9; Isa. 49:23; Mic. 7:17) and slinks low like
one. A return to dust was confirmed for the first readers by a simple
observation of what happens after burial. Humanity's origin from
dust suggests that reading the Eden story as an indication that we
were originally created to be immortal is to misunderstand it. "Dust
to dust" is an obvious fact of human impermanence (compare Eccl.
3:20), not a punishment that reversed initial human immortality.
However, the text also indicates that dust by itself was not enough to
make a human being. The human made from dust only becomes a
living being (like the animals, 2:19) when God breathes in life. The
intimate connection between life and breathing is again based on
simple observation. Babies enter life when they take their first breath;
dead people stop breathing.

The word *till* reiterates the close association between humans and the ground. At first, there is no one "to till the ground"(2:5). Humanity's first task of tilling is in the garden (2:15), but in the end they are sent forth "to till the ground" (3:23). The correspondence between the problem of 2:5 and the solution of 3:23 tells us that Genesis 2–3 is not just about humans, but also focuses on the earth and the trees and animals that come from the ground (2:9, 19). Creation took a step forward when the once fruitless ground came to have the farmers it needed to produce crops. This ecological note enriches our usual human-centered way of reading this story.

Garden occurs more than a dozen times throughout the story. You can find out what Israelites thought about gardens by looking up the word in a concordance and reading the passages designated there. This is a wonderful, hands-on way to get into the mental shoes of the original readers. Old Testament passages about gardens show them to be protected, luxuriant, nurturing, safe, and organized places:

- Gardens are protected with walls (Song 4:12). The Hebrew word for "garden" literally means "fenced."
- Gardens are well watered (Gen. 13:10; Deut. 11:10; Song 4:15).
- Gardens smell good and are sources of rich nourishment (Song 4:16).
- Gardens were part of the royal lifestyle (1 Kings 21:2; 2 Kings 25:4; Eccl. 2:5–6).
- Gardens represent the ultimate in riches and luxury (Ezek. 28:13; 31:8–9).
- Finally, gardens are for lovers, as the nine references in Song of Solomon illustrate.

Genesis 2–3 rests on the notion that tilling a garden is comparatively easy when compared to the frustration and heavy labor of ordinary farming described in 3:17–19. The word *Eden* apparently means "fertile because of water." The four rivers that flow from the garden and the resources of the lands they irrigate underscore Eden's richness (2:10–14).

Genesis 2:9, 15–17: Tree, Eat

Obviously, *tree* is a key word. The garden trees are pleasant to see and good for food (2:9). Woman recognizes these same features in the tree of knowledge (3:6). We are reminded twice that God commanded them not to eat of this tree (3:11, 17 referring to 2:16–17). Our experience with stories prepares us for what is to come, for any unexplained prohibition sets up tension in the reader's mind about whether the proscription will be violated, indeed an expectation that it will be. Will Pandora open the forbidden box? Most probably!

Looking carefully at the two trees, we see that both appear together in 2:9, but then the tree of life drops out of view until the very end. It only returns when God reminds us of its existence in 3:22–24. In other words, the *tree of life* frames the story at beginning and end, but the narrative in between spotlights the *tree of knowledge* instead (2:17; 3:3, 6, 11, 12, 17). Proverbs refers to a tree of life as an image of happiness and success (Prov. 3:18; 11:30; 13:12; 15:4). However, in Genesis 3:22 we discover that this is a very special tree of life, actually the tree of immortality. Because the tree of life disappears from the story between 2:9 and 3:22–24, we cannot know whether the pair has already been eating from it. However, the wording of 3:22 ("he might reach out his hand and take also") suggests that God intends to block this from happening for the first time (compare the wording of Gen. 22:10 and 2 Sam. 6:6).

The verb *eat* pervades the story, tying its elements together. Eating associates prohibition, disobedience, and consequence. It is the central element in God's permission and prohibition (2:16–17), Woman's conversation with Snake (3:1–5), and the act of human transgression (3:6, 11–13, 17). The result of this eating is a future that will consist of unpleasant eating for both Snake (3:14) and humanity (3:17–19). The "plants of the field" that do not exist in 2:5 materialize in 3:18 to make up the human diet. As the story closes, humanity is blocked from eating what would make immortality possible. The human situation has changed radically, from "you may freely eat of every tree" (2:16) to an exile that means we cannot "take also from the tree of life, and eat" (3:22).

Genesis 2:18–24: Helper as…Partner, Name, Flesh and Bone.

What do you suppose a *helper as…partner* would be like? A *helper* is one who assists, aids, and supports one in a task or situation. Possible synonyms are *colleague, associate, ally,* and *collaborator.* God can be our helper, as the psalmist reminds us (Ps. 33:20; 70:5; 115:10–11; 146:5). This means that there is nothing automatically subservient about being in the role of helper. Indeed, God is clearly looking for more than a subordinate assistant for Man. The animals could certainly have helped in the task of gardening if that was all that was needed. No, the words "not good…alone" in 2:18 indicate that this particular *helper* must be enough like Man to function as his *partner,* as one who corresponds to Man and prevents him from being alone. "As a partner" in Hebrew connotes correspondence and suitability, and Man recognizes this in Woman: "my bone, my flesh" (2:23). The expressions "clings" and "one flesh" in 2:24 go on to hint that Woman will be Man's *helper as…partner*, not just in gardening, but also in procreation. This becomes explicit in 3:20 and especially 4:1.

Name is another key word. Each of the four rivers is identified by name (2:11, 13, 14). Man names the animals (2:19), recognizes that Woman is the appropriate designation for his new partner (2:23), and after some delay, designates her as Eve (3:20). When he recognizes her as Woman, he effectively renames himself as male (2:23).

Man has begun our fundamental human adventure with language, classifying reality and building vocabulary. We shape the world around us and come to terms with it primarily through language. The first readers would not have seen Man's choice of names as arbitrary or accidental. Each name would have been considered appropriate to each animal's nature, an expression of the essence of what it means to be that animal. Foxes are foxy. Serpents are serpentine. Man becomes God's partner in creation, for in the thought world of the ancients, creation involved not just bringing things into existence, but also naming them (Gen. 1:5, 8, 10).

Man names the animals as soon as God presents them, but does not give Woman her personal name until 3:20, only after the first pair have made their fateful choice and God has announced the grim realities of their future existence. This order of events suggests that Eve's name, "Mother of All Living," serves as Man's comment on the difficulties described in 3:16–19. Perhaps Man (and the author) is affirming, "Nevertheless—life will go on and children will be born." The text gives us no clue as to whether we are to read Eve's name as an expression of faith, acquiescence, hope, or even defiance. But it clearly implies that expulsion from Eden is not the end of humanity's story but only the beginning.

What is implied by the designations "Eve" and "Mother of All Living"? Eve in Hebrew is *Ḥawwah,* "life giver." "Mother" is an honorific title in the Old Testament, as well as an expression of origin and priority. Eve is honored as mother of living things just as Deborah was revered with the title "mother in Israel" (Judg. 5:7). "Mother of All Living" also parallels the originators of various human activities depicted in Genesis 4:20–21. Jabal was the father (NRSV "ancestor") of all "who live in tents and have livestock"; and Jubal, the father of all those "who play the lyre and pipe." Woman is thus both first to give birth as a mother and the one who engenders all who live. The open-ended expression "*all* living" seems to go beyond the human species to indicate that Woman also has some relationship to the fertility of animals (2:19). This may be an echo of an artistic convention found in the cultures surrounding Israel, which pictured a goddess as standing in the midst of goats or other creatures as "Mistress of the Animals." Presumably, the original readers would have understood such subtle cultural messages better than we do.

Woman is Man's very *flesh* and *bone*. *Flesh* is an image of weakness in the Old Testament (Gen. 6:3); *bone* makes us think of strength. Taken together, the words imply that in all circumstances and in every way Woman and Man correspond. If you look in a concordance, you will discover that these two words together are used to express kinship and close relationship (Gen. 29:14; Judg. 9:2; 2 Sam. 5:1; 19:12–13). Woman's arrival means that a brand-new relational unit is created, one that transcends a person's family of origin or biological kinship. In spite of what is said in 2:24, a man in ancient Israel did not actually leave his parents' home to live with his wife. In fact, it was the other way around. Instead, "leaves his father and mother" seems to refer to psychological and social distance. In marriage a person turns away from childhood's emotional focus on parents and establishes a new and adult emotional orientation ("clings") centered on husband or wife.

Genesis 2:25–3:24: Naked, Shame, Know, Like, Cursed

Man and Woman are *naked* (2:25; 3:7, 10, 11). At first this is simply a neutral element: naked and not ashamed. Another possible translation would be "naked but not embarrassing to each other." A subtle wordplay in Hebrew links Snake to nakedness: the humans are naked *('êrōm),* but Snake is crafty *('ārûm;* 3:1). In Israelite culture nakedness could imply several different notions, among them vulnerability, shame, and sexuality. Vulnerability and perhaps shame are suggested by the human pair's reaction of covering, hiding, and fear (3:7, 10). Sexuality is suggested in their attempt to cancel out their nakedness by making *loincloths,* that is, something to cover their genitals. The upcoming story of Noah and his sons (9:18–27) shows the intense psychological and social power of nakedness in Israelite culture. Unashamed nakedness is also a characteristic of infancy (Job 1:21; Eccl. 5:15) and early childhood, a sign of innocence and immaturity.

In Israelite culture, *shame* and *honor* were the two poles of social existence. Shame grows out of dishonor. It is the embarrassment felt when some impropriety or social disgrace is perceived. However, shame can also be a positive thing, a turning away from being a bad person or doing bad things. As such it is the opposite of "shame-lessness."

Even a seemingly minor word such as *like* can serve as a key to meaning. In 3:5 Snake asserts that they will be *like* God, and later in 3:22 God reveals that this has in fact come true, "*like* one of us." But what sort of *like*-ness is meant? Of course, to be like God (or the "gods," see the NRSV note to 3:5) is hardly the same as actually being God or being equal to God in all things. Instead, Woman and Man are now like God in possessing a particular type of perception and discernment, "knowing good and evil." Human knowledge can be like that of God when it is perceptive and insightful. Consider what the wise woman of Tekoa says about David (2 Sam. 14:17) or the esteem in which Ahithophel was held as a counselor to kings (2 Sam. 16:23). The text suggests that curiosity is also an element in how we humans are like God. God brings the animals to Man out of curiosity—"to see what he would call them" (2:19). Doesn't Woman display the same characteristic as she considers the tree in response to Snake's claims about it?

Clearly there is something about us being like God that would only really become a problem if we were also immortal (3:22). Some sort of boundary between divine and human is in danger of being blurred, and God takes decisive action. We will encounter a similar concern on God's part in Genesis 6:1–3.

Did you notice that Snake is *cursed,* but that Woman and Man are not? For humans the curse is on the ground, not on either of them directly (3:17). Repetition of the key words *animals* and *wild animals/creatures* in 3:14 reminds us that Snake was one of those formed by God as a potential "helper as…partner" for Man (2:19–20; 3:1). Snake descends from being the most crafty of animals to being the most cursed of animals, suffering a "low-down," "stomped-on" existence.

Step Five: Opposites and Contrasts

What opposing or contrasting pairs of words or ideas are present? Sometimes, listing key words or concepts in opposing pairs helps us understand the fundamental movement of a narrative. Try it with the Eden story.

You probably have come up with some of these: good and evil, life and death, man and woman, naked and clothed. A list that includes ideas and concepts might include then and now, two sexes over against one flesh, and inside the garden in contrast to outside it. Humanity is in three interlocking paired relationships: human and animal (including Snake), human and earth, and human and God. I will limit myself to observations on the contrasting pairs man/woman and good/evil.

Man and Woman

The key words *man* (as a human being, *ʾādām*), *man* (as a human adult male, *ʾîš*), and *woman* (*ʾiššah*) are difficult to untangle (see "Hebrew Word List"). Let's begin with *man* as a human being.

In 2:7, God takes *ʾādām* from the *ʾădāmah* (ground). *ʾĀdām* normally means "human" in general without regard to gender, so that at first this character seems to coordinate with the gender-neutral English word "mankind." However, this first human in due course develops directly into the male in the story. This is clear from 2:21–25 and then 3:8–12, 17, 20. Even so, in 3:18–19 and 22–24 what is said of *ʾādām* is also true of all humans. So Man (*ʾādām*) plays a dual role, both as the specifically male human being, whose partner is Woman, and as a representation of humanity as a whole. Making the central figure of the creation story a "hu-*man*" who is simultaneously a male "he-*man*" reflects the male-centered attitudes of ancient Israel.

Eventually the designation Man (*ʾādām*) segues into the proper name Adam. Translators tend to differ about when this switch takes place. The KJV uses Adam as a name for the first time in 2:19, and the JPSV does so in 2:20. The RSV starts at 3:17, but the NRSV waits as long as possible, until 4:25.

Woman (*ʾiššah*) is translated *wife* when connected with a possessive pronoun (2:24, 25; 3:8, 17, 20, 21). The noun *Woman* results from a wordplay that expresses Man's recognition of her origin: *ʾiššah* (woman) taken out of *ʾîš* (man as human male; see the NRSV footnote to 2:23). However, this act of naming cuts two ways, for in designating his new partner as Woman, Man is at the same time giving himself a new label. Now he is not only *ʾādām*, the first human, but also *ʾîš*, man who is male in relationship to and partnership with woman. What it means to be human has changed decisively. Woman proves to be the decisive factor in the story. In Genesis 2, she is needed to achieve a good and complete creation. In Genesis 3, her choice becomes the catalyst for humanity's transition out of Eden into our present world.

Since we are not told anything different, we readers must assume that before Woman appeared on the scene, Man was potentially and physically male, but now he has become a male actually and functionally as well. He remains the same in that the human ʾādām, whose rib was removed (2:21) and to whom God brings Woman (2:22), is identical with the male human being (ʾîš) from whose body Woman was taken (2:23). But Man is also now radically different, not merely because he is missing a rib, but because God has confronted him with a matching female other. She is a "helper as...partner" of identical bone and flesh. The expression "taken from" implies that she is both the same as Man and separate from Man. "At last," he exclaims! This Woman who was once part of his own subjective self is now an object of his appreciation. From now on, 2:24 tells us, the typical male human (ʾîš) will abandon home and cling to a female human (ʾiššah). As the story continues, Man is both ʾîš and ʾādām. He is ʾîš when he is related to Woman as "her husband" (3:6, 16), but remains ʾādām when Woman is related to him as "his wife" (3:8, 9, 12, 20, 21) and when he serves as the representation of all humanity (3:17, 22–24).

In Genesis 3 Woman comes into her own. She speaks on behalf of her husband and herself ("we," 3:2). She sees, takes, gives (3:6), and is addressed individually by God (3:16). Yet the text takes a strange turn after 3:16–17. Woman begins to disappear behind words addressed to and about Man as the representation of all humanity. In 3:18–19 and 22–24, what is said of Man (ʾādām) is true of all humans, not just of males. It is not just the male who engages in agricultural toil or dies, or who has become like God and is driven out from Eden. Thus Man (ʾādām) is used to refer to humanity as a whole both at the beginning and at the end of the Eden story.

Twenty-first–century readers tend to find this unsettling, even annoying. The Eden narrative is relentlessly male-centered. Man as male remains the center of attention throughout: "not good that *man* should be alone," "helper as *his* partner," "brought her to the *man*," "out of *man* this one was taken," "a *man* leaves," "called *his* wife's name Eve," "drove out the *man*." It is only in 3:1–15 that matters are more evenhanded. The sexism of the Old Testament may be distressing, but it is a fact of life; and we must learn to live with it and negotiate around it.

Knowing Good and Evil

A controversial complex of key ideas are communicated by the repeated phrase *knowing* (or *knowledge of) good and evil* (2:9, 17; 3:5,

22). An immediate problem is caused by the English word *evil,* which readers will likely understand in terms of moral evil or cosmic evil. But evil in Hebrew refers more broadly to anything disastrous, injurious, or detrimental. It would be better to translate the phrase as "good and bad" or "that which is beneficial and harmful." If you look up this phrase in a concordance and study the passages indicated, you will find that it describes the ability to discriminate between what helps and what hurts, what has the potential to enhance life or to spoil it.

Knowing good and evil is the capacity for discernment that one acquires when one grows up. Those referred to in Deuteronomy 1:39 are too young to have it, and the youngster portrayed in Isaiah 7:15–16 will achieve it as he grows up (compare Isa. 8:4). In 2 Samuel 19:35 the speaker suggests that he has lost this capacity because he is too old, in his second childhood (NRSV "can I discern what is pleasant and what is not?" is literally "do I know between good and bad?"). Such perceptive discrimination is an ability that kings need to have (2 Sam. 14:17). Solomon prays for it because he thinks of himself as being as immature as a child (1 Kings 3:9).

These passages suggest that *good and evil* are not so much *what* is known but a way of knowing. Knowing good and evil signifies an effective discrimination between what is helpful and harmful to life, between what leads to happy consequences and harmful ones. Man and Woman gain this knowledge by seeing things in a new way through newly "opened eyes" (3:5, 7). If you work with a concordance, you will discover that when someone's eyes are opened he or she experiences revival (2 Kings 4:35) and a perception of what had previously been hidden (Gen. 21:19; 2 Kings 6:17, 20; Isa. 6:10). When their eyes are opened, Man and Woman recognize differences they had not perceived before. They *see* they are different from each other (again, loincloths!) and thus *know* they are naked.

Perhaps it is precisely Woman's immature lack of the capacity to know good and evil that leads her astray in the first place. Her perceptions about the tree are not completely off the mark (3:6). It may have been good for food and was certainly pleasant to look at (compare 2:9). Wisdom is a goal worth striving for. But she misperceives the tree's long-term harmful potential for alienation from God. Her childlike lack of discerning perception (to say nothing of that of Man) leads her into a choice that results in her acquiring precisely the adult insight that might have prevented her misjudgment in the first place. What irony!

The opposites *good* and *evil* also imply comprehensive knowledge—from good things to bad things, and everything in between. Of course, this cannot mean that humans could ever know absolutely everything. The first pair may now know they are naked, but they are hardly omniscient, since they cannot even make proper clothes for themselves! The point may be that our human capacity for perception and discrimination embraces all areas of life, not just morality or ethics. It is an inclusive discrimination across all categories of what can be good or bad.

Was Woman wrong when she interpreted the tree as being able to "make one wise" (3:6)? In the Old Testament, wisdom is a capacity for understanding that leads to success and the mastery of life. Sirach 17:7 (in the Apocrypha) equates God's revelation of "good and evil" with knowledge and understanding. It is hard to see that knowing the difference between good and evil could be an entirely bad thing for us. To choose something bad because you thought it was good would be completely unwise. It is true wisdom to know that all things have a potential for both good and evil and that human knowledge is ambivalent and can elevate life or endanger it.

Read in this way, the story of Eden suggests that the only way that the human race could have moved from oblivious childhood to adult maturity was by acquiring the capacity to discriminate between good and bad. However, the story also indicates that this essential attainment was not without cost. This new capacity to know good and evil resulted in shame and fear, with Adam and Eve covering their bodies and hiding from God. Moreover, the very knowledge we need to function as mature and autonomous humans brings with it the knowledge of death (3:19). Such perception and discrimination is a capability that we humans share with God.

Step Seven: Patterns and Structures

What arrangements or patterns give structure to the language and movement of the text? Look for repeated words or phrases. Look for "envelopes" or "bookends," concentric structures, and wordplays. Analyze how pronouns are used and how characters are addressed.

Ancient writers and readers took great delight in verbal patterns. Learning to recognize these helps us experience the energy and internal connections present in a text. However, seeing these patterns is not easy at first. Unless you have already had some experience as a biblical interpreter, it may be best for you to put off trying to do this step on your own until you have read my observations. You can try your hand at it when we get to Cain and Abel (chapter 4).

Poetry and Reversals

The heightened language of poetry emphasizes certain sentences, highlighting them against the prose background as elevated speech. Old Testament poetry is marked by the repetition of parallel lines. The NRSV prints as poetry Man's first exclamation about Woman (2:23) and the patterned, repetitious punishments of 3:14–19. However, careful reading uncovers some other examples of poetic language. The narrative begins in 2:5 with a rhythmical poetic couplet:

> when no plant of the field was yet in the earth
> and no herb of the field had yet sprung up

Woman's thoughts as she views the tree are also poetic (3:6 translated to highlight the Hebrew word order):

> that good was the tree for food
> and that a delight was it for the eyes
> and that desirable was the tree for making wise

Patterns of reversal are often used to call attention to textual relationships. Thus the phrase "the heavens and the earth" in the first half of 2:4 is reversed into "the earth and the heavens" in the second half of the verse, indicating that a new story is about to begin. Snake cleverly reverses the order of God's prohibition so that "every tree of the garden" (2:16b) and "you shall not eat" (2:17a) is turned into "you shall not eat from any tree in the garden" (3:1b). In this way Snake induces Woman to explain what she understands the true situation to be. In 3:4–5, Snake reverses the order of 2:17 in two ways to cast doubts on God's motives and veracity:

> knowledge of good and evil / you shall die
> you will not die / knowing good and evil
>   and
> in the day that you eat of it / you shall die
> you will not die / when (Hebrew: "on a day") you eat of it your
>   eyes will be opened.

Later on, God reverses the sequence of eating (first Woman, then Man, 3:6) by interrogating Man first and Woman second (3:9–13).

Envelopes, Repetitions, and Concentric Structures

"Envelope" or "bookend" patterns enclose and unify material through repetition at the beginning and end. Thus 2:7–8 is held together and highlighted by "God formed man" at the beginning and "man whom he had formed" at the end. The phrase "helper as his partner" (at the end of both v. 18 and v. 20) envelopes and holds together the failed search for such a helper among the animals. In a similar way, Man's poetic exclamation about Woman is enveloped by "this one" coming at the beginning and the end (in the original Hebrew word order):

> *This one* at last is bone of my bone and flesh of my flesh, *this one* shall be called Woman for from Man was taken *this one*. (2:28)

Likewise, the notices about contrasting reactions to being naked in 2:25 ("were both naked, and were not ashamed") and 3:7 ("they knew they were naked") provide a "before and after" framework around the dialogue between Snake and Woman in 3:1–6.

A more complex pattern emerges in the reciprocal movement within 3:19:

> until you *return* to the *ground,*
>> for out of *it* you were *taken;*
> you are *dust,*
>> and to *dust* you shall *return.*

If we look for wider patterns and shapes, we discover that the whole story is held together by a complex series of framing elements repeated at the beginning and then again at the end:

- There is "no one to till the ground" (2:5) at the start, but at the end humanity is sent out "to till the ground" (3:23).
- The tree of life disappears after 2:9 and only reappears at the end in 3:22, 24.
- "Knowledge of good and evil" at the beginning (2:9) is paralleled by "knowing good and evil" near the end (3:22)
- "Put him in the garden of Eden" (2:15) is balanced and reversed by "sent him forth from the garden of Eden" (3:23)

A special kind of iteration commonly found in the Old Testament is a repetition that restarts a story after a parenthetical section has interrupted it. A textbook example of such a "resumptive repetition" is present in 2:8 and 2:15. The background information about rivers in 2:10–14 does not really advance the plot and could easily be ignored by the reader. So when that background paragraph is finished, verse 15 picks up the main story line again by repeating and reversing elements from verse 8:

> a garden in Eden / there he put the man (v. 8)
> took the man and put him / in the garden of Eden (v. 15)

Verse 15 then moves the story forward by going on to state the purpose for this: "to till…and keep it."

Another resumptive repetition is obscured by the word order required by English translation. In 3:11, God begins the announcement of negative consequences with an accusatory question directed at Man (in the literal word order of the original Hebrew): "From the tree of which I commanded you not to eat / have you eaten?" However, God then temporarily bypasses Man and speaks first to Snake and then to Woman (3:13–16). When God goes back to address Man once more, this return to the original subject is picked up in verse 17 with a reversal of verse 11: "You…have eaten / of the tree about which I commanded you 'You shall not eat of it.'"

Parallel patterns coordinate the first transgression in 3:6 with the defensive human responses in 3:13 and 3:12:

> she took and she ate / Snake tricked and I ate
> she gave and he ate / you gave…she gave and I ate

Old Testament writers had a special fondness for concentric patterns of repeated themes and vocabulary. Ancient readers apparently noticed these arrangements without difficulty, but we moderns must be especially alert to detect them. One such pattern of concentric themes emerges as Man twice gives his partner a name:

A. shall be called Woman—2:23
  B. a man leaves (explains marriage)—2:24
    C. both were naked but not ashamed—2:25
      X. she ate, he ate—3:6
    C'. they knew that they were naked—3:7
  B'. to dust you shall return (explains burial)—3:19b
A'. named his wife (woman) Eve—3:20

This arrangement draws our attention to the central action of rebellious eating in 3:6.

Careful attention to repetitions and parallels in a more general sense can uncover a great deal. If we look at expressions of motion with the prepositions "from" and "to/unto," we notice that there are two separations in the first part of the story: Man is formed *from* the dust of the ground (2:7) and Woman is taken *from* Man (2:22). But there are also reverse movements of (re)union. Woman is brought *to* Man (2:22) and her desire is *to* him (3:16, literally in the original Hebrew). In death, Humanity returns *to* ground and dust (3:19). This pattern draws a parallel between the (re)union of sexual attraction and the (re)union of death.

The characters in 3:1–19 appear in an artistically pleasing sequence. In the episode of transgression (3:1–6), they are introduced in the order Snake, Woman, Man. This is reversed in the defensive response to God's interrogation (3:12–13) as Man points to Woman and then Woman points to Snake. Then the announcement of consequences (3:14–19) goes back to the original sequence: Snake, Woman, Man.

Pronouns and Address

An analysis of pronouns and how characters are addressed can sometimes be revealing. Modern English translations can create problems, however. Hebrew uses different second person ("you") pronouns for singular and plural. English once did the same thing, using "thou," "thee," and "thy" for singular and "ye," "you," and "your" for plural. Here is one place where your old *King James Bible* can still be useful, since it differentiates between second person plural and singular: "Ye shall not eat" (3:3) in contrast to, "Hast thou eaten?" (3:11).

The pronouns in Genesis 3 indicate an overall degeneration from human community in 3:1–8 to human alienation in 3:10–13. Snake refers to both humans by using plural "you" (3:1, 4–5), even though it is speaking directly to the Woman. Earlier, Man had spoken in terms of "my" and "I" (2:23), but now Woman uses the language of community with "we" (3:2). Like Snake, she substitutes a plural "you" for the original singular "you" when repeating God's prohibition (3:3, referring to 2:16–17). The writer continues to describe Man and Woman as a mutual pair as they sew their loincloths and hide (3:7–8). But from that point on their unity breaks down into alienation. God begins this by asking, "Where are you?" using the singular (v. 9). The humans defend themselves, not in terms of "we," but with a repeated "I." The communal "they heard" and "they hid" of 3:8 degenerates into Man's individualized "I heard" and "I hid" in 3:10. Both Man and Woman conclude their confessions with an isolating "I ate" in 3:12 and 13. In sharp contrast to his delighted description of Woman in 2:24 ("my bones…my flesh"), Man uses objective language ("the woman") to distance himself from her in 3:12. Human community has dissolved under the pressure of God's displeasure.

Sources

The Mesopotamian stories of *Enuma Elish, Gilgamesh,* and *Atrahasis* are available in Victor H. Matthews and Don C. Benjamin,

Old Testament Parallels, revised edition (New York: Paulist Press, 1997), 19–40. I am indebted to Ellen van Wolde, *A Semiotic Analysis of Genesis 2–3,* SSN 25 (Assen: Van Gorcum, 1989) and Beverly J. Stratton, *Out of Eden: Reading, Rhetoric, and Ideology in Genesis 2–3,* JSOTSup 208 (Sheffield: Sheffield Academic Press, 1995).

CHAPTER 3

The Kindergarten of Eden
Genesis 2–3 continued

In chapter 2 we practiced looking at the impact of individual words and themes, along with smaller verbal shapes and patterns. As we did so, the theme of growing up and maturation emerged at several points.

The Eden story has traditionally been understood as a narrative about humanity's first sin and its destructive consequences on our relationship to God and the earth. But the theme of human development and maturation is also present. Man and Woman begin as naïve and innocent "babes in the wood," but as their adventure in the "kindergarten of Eden" progresses, they develop into mature adults. They encounter sexuality, rebel against God's parental authority, and gain new insight and perception. They discover the harsh realities of adult drudgery and the inequitable situation of women in a man's world. God gives them clothes suitable for adult life and sends them off into the wider world.

In this chapter, we will look at the design of the Eden story as a whole. We will begin by going back to read the story one more time. Please reread it section by section while I make comments and observations along the way.

Going over the Story Again

Genesis 2:4–17

Genesis 2:4b-7 is really a single long sentence in Hebrew. "In the day" and "when" in 2:4–6 set the stage for the "then" of the main actions described in 2:7: God formed and breathed, and Man emerged. There was no plant or herb because as yet there was no rain and no farmer. The lack of rain was not really the problem, because water was rising up from below the earth. God forms Man in response to the other problem—there was "no one to till the ground" (2:5).

The story takes a twist when Man is not put in a position to till "the ground," but put into a garden instead (2:8). We do not find out Man's purpose for being there until 2:15 ("to till it and keep it"). "East" refers to the perspective of the reader and writer, that is, Eden is east of Palestine. The background paragraph 2:10–14 about rivers delays the plot, which only moves forward again with 2:15.

Genesis 2:10–14 starts with what is unfamiliar and moves to what is better known. Pishon and Gihon form a similar sounding pair with identical vowel sounds, but are otherwise unknown, mentioned as rivers nowhere else. The paragraph then moves to the well-known Tigris and Euphrates. The amount of information given for each river decreases. We are told most about the Pishon, and nothing but the name of the familiar Euphrates. These rivers illustrate Eden's richness and mark off the four regions of the world known to the ancient Israelites. They also connect Eden to the geography (Cush, Assyria, Havilah) and economy (gold, jewels, aromatic resins) of that world. (Did you look up "bdellium" in your Bible dictionary?) Rivers and coastal seas were the trade routes of the ancient world.

When the trees are introduced in 2:9, the text spotlights the tree of life. But the prohibition in 2:17 shifts our attention to the other tree. The tree of life disappears until 3:22. Are God's words about death a threat of capital punishment or a gracious, protective warning? Is this like a cautionary notice put up at a hazardous location: "Deadly Danger. Keep Out!"? The unconditional immediacy of "in the day that you eat" will cause us to ask some hard questions later on.

Genesis 2:18–25

Rather than immediately pursuing the matter of this prohibition, the story takes another twist to deal with the predicament that Man is alone. This explains when and why God created animals and why animals are similar to us in some ways. It also brings Snake into the picture (3:1).

I can't help thinking of Tarzan, for whom life with the animals was not really enough and who needed Jane to become a fully grown-up man ("Me Tarzan. You Jane.") Woman is the perfect solution to Man's solitude, as his delighted and poetic outburst makes clear, in essence: "Me Man. You Woman." Some assert that by naming Woman, Man is claiming domination over her. Perhaps so, but there are many places where name giving has nothing to do with claims of superior authority (Gen. 4:1, for example). The explanatory "therefore" of 2:24 breaks off the flow of the story for a moment and points forward into our present-day world.

The reader knows that "naked, and...not ashamed" (2:25) is not a normal or stable condition. Obviously, something will have to happen to get humanity dressed.

Genesis 3:1–13

Now that animals and especially Woman are on the scene, the plot turns back to the question raised by the prohibition in 2:17. Nakedness leads directly into the new paragraph begun by 3:1 through a wordplay. They are naked *('êrōm),* but Snake is crafty *('ārûm).* The text tells us nothing about Snake's motives. We only know what Snake says, not why.

The same Hebrew word can mean both "any" and "all," which makes Snake's question in 3:1 misleading. Snake's words could mean, "Is any tree forbidden?" or, "Are all the trees forbidden?" Woman cannot answer this crafty question with a simple yes or no, and so Snake forces her to reflect and elaborate.

In 3:2–3, Woman reports on what God said in 2:17. Let us compare the two versions. Woman modifies what she has heard secondhand from Man. She converts the original "you singular" situation of 2:17 into a "you plural" address. She knows God's prohibition applies to her and not just to Man. She also adds "nor shall you touch it." Is her addition of "don't touch" a reasonable extra precaution or an irresolute perversion of God's original command? In either case, her enhanced version of the prohibition communicates how tempting this forbidden fruit has become for her. In 2:9 the tree of life was in the "midst of the garden," but now Woman identifies the tree of knowledge instead as the one "in the middle of the garden." This tree has become the focus of her attention.

In 3:4–5, Snake operates as the original "spin doctor," telling the truth, but not the whole truth. They would not die that very day, but in the end they would. They would become like God in knowing good and evil, but would never really become completely like God. Snake hints that God's motives are unworthy. Perhaps a better translation for "your eyes will be opened" (3:5) is "your eyes will open up." The NRSV note to 3:5 informs us that the Hebrew word for "God" as a proper name is the same as the plural common noun for "gods."

Genesis 3:7 allows us a glimpse into Woman's thoughts. Her act is not completely thoughtless or impulsive, but based on some reflection. She does not build her perspective about the tree on what Snake has said, but makes her own observations about its evident physical, aesthetic, and intellectual advantages.

Disobedience is followed by enlightenment and discovery (3:6– 7). Man and Woman together ("the eyes of both") make the first discovery, namely that they are naked. Nothing whatsoever is said about guilt in their reaction. Instead, their behavior is caused by newly opened eyes that give them a new capacity for observation and knowledge (3:7) and by the fear in God's presence that this new knowledge has produced (3:10). The restricted coverage provided by loincloths signals that this crisis over nudity has to do with sexuality and sexual difference. These loincloths do not really solve the problem of self-consciousness, because Man continues to be afraid because of his nakedness (3:10).

Modern readers will probably be uncomfortable with the depiction of God strolling about in the breezy cool of the day, but we have already run into God's direct physical interaction with earthly things in 2:7 and 21–22. God interrogates the disobedient pair, starting with Man, who quickly lets slip the momentous and damning truth that he knows he is naked. God's pointed follow-up questions snap the trap shut: Who told you? Have you eaten?

Genesis 3:14–25

Some understand 3:14–19 as punishments caused directly by God. Following this reasoning the NAB and NJPS translate 3:17 as "cursed be the ground." Other interpreters see these verses as God's disclosure of the inevitable consequences of disobedience. Thus the REB translates this as "the earth will be cursed."

God's speech in 3:14–19 is poetry, elevated language used for serious matters. Woman is the common factor in all three sections of God's speech (3:15, 16, 17). God treats each of the offenders differently. Snake is not questioned, only cursed (either "among" the other animals [NRSV], "more than" other animals [NJPS], or "from" them [NAB]). God gives reasons for what is announced to Snake and Man ("because you have done this"; "because you have listened…and have eaten"), but gives no reason for what Woman will experience. Snake is cursed, but Woman and Man are not. Instead, the ground is cursed as regards human agriculture.

The word translated "pangs" in 3:16 is the same as that translated "toil" in 3:17. Some translate, "I will greatly increase your toils and your pregnancies," referring to a wider scope of Woman's life than simply procreation. In the Old Testament the fulfillment achieved in motherhood was much more central to women's lives and consciousness than it is among us (compare 19:30–38). From now on, says God, where Woman finds her greatest fulfillment is also where she will experience pain and subordination.

The statements in 3:17b-19 (and vv. 22–24) obviously apply to both sexes, not just to males. Men and women both die, and agriculture was the task of both sexes in the ancient world. Perhaps these particular consequences are announced specifically to Man because he was taken from the ground (2:7) and assigned the task of tilling it (2:15). "Listen to the voice of" (3:17) is a Hebrew idiom that means obey. Man's transgression was not in paying attention to what a mere woman said (the traditional sexist interpretation), but rather in listening to anyone, even his spouse, instead of obeying God. "Bread" (3:19) points to agricultural life; fruit is no longer at the center of the human diet.

The wording of 3:19 ("until") suggests that return to the ground is more a blessed release from a life of toil than a fearful punishment. There is nothing unexpected or horrifying about this dissolution. The full circle of "from dust…to dust" has been accomplished. The Old Testament views death at the end of a long and satisfying life as a positive achievement (Gen. 15:15; 35:29).

Having achieved a new level of perception and knowledge, Man and Woman have become in some limited ways like God and the subordinate heavenly beings (3:22). For this reason, open-ended life without any end in view must be denied them. To possess godlike knowledge, while also obtaining godlike immortality, would encroach on what must remain reserved only for God and the divine beings. The tree that would make immortality possible is made permanently unattainable. Artists like to portray an angel brandishing a sword to illustrate 3:24, but two separate security systems are intended: several guardian cherubim *and* a self-activated sword. Humanity is sent forth to till the ground, putting an end to the deficiency in the earth's ecology described in 2:6.

The Order of Creation and the Target of Temptation

In earlier periods, when society and religion simply assumed that women were inferior to men in rationality and achievement, the order of events in the Eden story was presumed to support that male-centered worldview. Because Woman was created second, she was of secondary worth, merely a by-product from the fundamental male prototype. It was assumed that Snake directed its questions to Woman because she was an easier target for temptation. Her weakness and inconstancy were chiefly responsible for humanity's present condition.

However, sometimes we can learn a great deal about a story if we try to tell it in a different way or in a different order. When we attempt to retell the Eden story in reverse order, we discover that the existing plot sequence is really the only one that will work.

The Order of Creation

First, if Woman had been formed first and Man derived from her, this would merely describe the normal process of birth. Man would be Woman's child. Rather than Man and Woman both being special creations of God, Man would be merely derivative of Woman. Worse, the notion of First Man being born from First Woman would immediately lead the ancient reader to the question of paternity. Was God the father? If not, then who? The cultures surrounding Israel told stories of divine sexual activity with humans, and this is even described in Genesis 6:1–4. However, Israel's God did not engage in sex, and such a notion would have been considered extremely dangerous by the biblical authors.

Second, the biblical order of events means that Woman's origin can be unique. Her creation can be described as the result of the same attention to purpose and hands-on divine effort as that invested in Man. Woman's origin and specific design is the product of God's thoughtful response to the requirements of human companionship. God makes her by building something up around a foundational bone taken from Man's side, in the way that ancient people sometimes made statuettes by shaping clay around a bone core. Her inner framework (bone) is derived from Man and so identical, but her outer shaping is God's direct, hands-on work. Thus in 2:23 Man recognizes her both as a distinctly different "this one" and a delightfully similar "bone of my bones and flesh of my flesh." Perhaps God takes Woman from Man's *side* (a better translation than "rib") to express the "side-by-side" nature of human marriage. Couples stand side by side and walk side by side. Ancient Egyptian and Mesopotamian statues portray husband and wife standing or sitting in just this posture.

Third, both distinctive creation events are absolutely necessary for the story to perform its function, because each act of creation leads directly to a critical aspect of human existence. God forms Man from ground and dust, which points to the reality that men and women work the soil and dissolve back into dust at death. God builds Woman from Man's side, which points to shared companionship, sexual attraction, and marriage. The quest for a "helper as…partner" also serves to introduce animals onto the scene.

Fourth, if the order of creation were reversed, the wordplay of *ʾiššah* taken from *ʾiš* (2:23; Woman taken from Man-as-male) would no longer be possible. Israelite culture believed that universal truths were often hidden in the structure of language. In the popular mind, *ʾiššah* was assumed to be an expansion of the simpler word *ʾiš* (although this is not actually true). The availability of such a pun in Hebrew would automatically cause people to assume that Woman had once been taken from Man.

The Target of Temptation

Why is Woman the object of Snake's temptations? Is Woman being viewed as weaker and more vulnerable than Man? Again, trying to tell the story in a different way suggests that the storyteller had little choice in this matter. If Snake had spoken first to Man, the story would not work as it should. Woman and Man could not both be held fully responsible for what happened. The reader would be encouraged to hold Man entirely responsible and let Woman off the hook.

First, Man had heard the prohibition of 2:17 personally and directly. He would presumably have answered Snake with an "I" rather than a "we" (see 3:2) and thus have left Woman out of the prohibition. Indeed, if Snake and Man were conversing about this, how would we ever learn that Woman was also aware of God's ban on eating?

Second, readers would naturally assume that wives would obey their husbands and follow their lead. If Man had taken the fruit first and then given it to Woman, her culpability would be diminished or eliminated. Eating would no longer have been a completely free choice for her. Indeed, if she were to go on to defend herself in terms of what Man says in 3:12 ("my husband gave it to me"), it would be a perfectly reasonable excuse!

For the narrative to work, Woman must dialogue with Snake while Man is silent. Woman must choose to eat before Man does. By telling the story in this particular way, the author insists that Woman was capable of sophisticated thought and could make independent choices. These are notions that the original male-dominated readership may not have accepted easily. Woman and Man are portrayed as being equally responsible for the choices they make. In fact, in comparison with Woman, Man seems to be something of a pushover! No serpentine trickery or scrutiny of the tree's attractions is needed for him. He acquiesces silently: she gives, he eats—end of story.

Woman was made after Man and was the one whom Snake tempted and who first ate the fruit. These narrative features were never intended to indicate Woman's secondary status or her special gullibility. Rather, they tell a story of human equality, free choice, and shared moral responsibility.

Step Eight: Plot Movement

A plot is movement from *problem* to *solution.* In most stories, the main problem is usually complicated by several sub-problems that need to find resolution before the story is over. Cinderella begins as an unappreciated beauty sitting in the ashes, and her predicament is ultimately resolved when she marries Prince Charming. But along the way other obstacles must be overcome before the plot can reach its goal: the hostility of her stepsisters, no dress, no coach, the need for the prince to rediscover her after she flees at midnight.

One of the most rewarding steps in the interpretive process calls on us to *describe the movement of the plot. What parts move the story forward, and what parts provide background or delay resolution?* "Movement of the plot" refers to the way a story moves through stages from problem to resolution. Complex stories may have subplots in which other problems come to resolution along with the main plot. I usually find it helpful to draw a flow chart or diagram of the way a story moves.

Background and Delay

Stories have main actions that take place in the *foreground* (Red Riding Hood meets the wolf) and *background* information that sets the stage for the action ("Once upon a time there was a brave little girl who lived near the forest"). Background information at the start of a narrative is called *exposition.* Genesis 2:4–6 is obviously exposition, informing us about when and under what circumstances the following story will take place. Storytellers and writers use *delay* to create tension and reader interest. Anyone experienced with stories knows that an emphatic prohibition often leads to a violation of it. (Remember Lot's wife, Gen. 19:17, 26!)

The prohibition is introduced in 2:17, but the writer delays the question of its violation for an extended period. The story first explores the four rivers and then recounts the creation of animals and Woman. Only then does it move back to the question of forbidden fruit. The paragraph about the four rivers creates a delay between Man's placement in the garden with the two trees (2:8–9) and our learning why Man was put there and what Man's relationship with the trees will be (2:15–17). A similar delay appears near the end of the story. God's pronouncements about humanity's grim life in a world that is certainly not Eden (3:16–19) leads the reader to expect that Man and Woman will be expelled from there. However, that climatic event is delayed for a couple of verses while Eve gets her name and God makes clothing.

Biblical writers sometimes wait to reveal information until the reader needs to know it. This is called *delayed exposition*. Thus we know from the start that there is something called a "tree of life" in the garden (2:9), but it is not until the very end that we readers are told that this tree is the source of immortality (3:22). Again, it is only in 3:6 that we learn that Man was with Woman during her previous discussion with Snake, and it is only in 3:17 that the writer reveals that Woman spoke to Man when she gave him the fruit.

Plots and Subplots

The introduction to the primary plot of the Eden story appears in 2:5: plants and herbs were "not yet" because "there was no one to till the ground." This is clearly intended to be an unfavorable situation. God follows up with corrective action by forming a human from the very ground that requires someone to till it (2:7). Yet (for reasons unexplained), this human being is put into a fertile garden "to till it" instead (2:9, 15). Ultimately this problem is solved when the humans are driven from Eden "to till the ground" (3:23). However, a number of intervening instabilities and crises must be dealt with before this conclusion can be realized, and many elements of present-day human existence emerge in the process.

THE PRIMARY PLOT

This *primary plot* is set up in 2:4–9, 15 and resolved in 3:22–24. It reaches its *climax* or dramatic high point in 3:23 when the humans are expelled to till the ground. Verbal clues point to the correspondence between initial problem and eventual solution. Thus "no plant of the field" in 2:5 is picked up and reversed by "eat the plants of the field" in 3:18. "Put him in the garden of Eden" in 2:15 is cancelled out by "sent him forth from the garden of Eden" in 3:23. Genesis 3:24 then explores the consequences of this climactic expulsion, what students of literature would call the *denouement.* This primary plot line is centered on the requirements of the ground. Human beings are not the focal point of the story understood in this way. They are a means that God has devised for solving an ecological concern! Human existence cannot be divorced from the destiny of the earth.

THE SUBPLOTS

Nestled within this main plot movement are six *subplots* in which we humans come more directly under the spotlight. These subplots are not completely independent, of course, but are interlinked with the main plot. First, the prohibition of forbidden fruit, Snake's enticements, and the humans' transgression lead to expulsion, so that the goal of the main plot can be met. Second, human solitude leads to the creation of animals and to human community. Third, a state of nakedness changes to one of being clothed. Fourth, humans move from a state of harmony with each other, the ground, animals, and God to a state of alienation. Fifth, humans move from a state of unperceptive and childlike naiveté to "knowing good and evil," and as a result are excluded from immortality. Sixth, there is a reciprocal movement of separation and reunion. Let us look at these subplots each in turn.

From Prohibition through Transgression to Consequences

This subplot appears in 2:16–17 and 3:1–19. If the ground is to be tilled, then life in the garden cannot be the end of the story. Indeed, for all its rich and well-watered pleasantness, we readers soon suspect that Eden will prove to be an unstable situation. Because we know human nature and the outcome of other familiar stories about prohibitions, we tend to expect that the command of 2:17 will be violated. This expected violation does not happen immediately, however, but only after the elements of community and ambiguity have been added to the situation. The creation of Woman means that no longer one, but two, humans stand before the forbidden tree. These two are engaged in a relational community involving sexual attraction and difference, something that multiplies the complexities of the decision they will make. Ambiguity emerges in the form of Snake with its questions and half-true observations. The high points of this subplot occur in 3:6 ("she ate, he ate") and God's penetrating question "Have you eaten?" (3:11) It concludes with the expulsion of the human pair as a consequence of transgressing the prohibition. Ironically, humans have moved from one divinely imposed limit that operated in free will ("of the tree of the knowledge of good and evil you shall not eat" [2:17]) to another limit imposed upon us, one that we no longer have the freedom to violate ("he might…take also from the tree of life, and eat" [3:22]).

This subplot connects to the main plot. Woman's interpretation of the tree's qualities (3:6) links back to the main plot as she revisits the original description of the trees of Eden (2:9). Expulsion from Eden connects to the main plot's ultimate concern to provide someone "to till the ground," and the consequences of transgression described in 3:17–19 also relate to humanity's agricultural assignment.

From Solitude through Animals to Human Community

Transgression is encouraged by a shrewd and questioning animal and happens in the context of human community. These two factors are the outcomes of a subplot that unfolds primarily in 2:18–25. God recognizes the problem of human solitude. Man is alone, and that is not good. God's response to this leads to the appearance of animals and the beginnings of human language. Resolution to the solitude problem comes when God builds Woman and presents her to Man. The situation changes from "alone" (2:18) to human companionship, signaled by "cling" (2:24), "man and his wife" (2:25), "we" (3:2), "her husband…with her" (3:6), "both" (3:7). In this original partnership of mutual openness, nakedness produces no disturbance or threat.

From Nakedness to Clothing

However, we know that human community inevitably brings with it antagonism and distance. Nakedness (2:25) is our first hint that this initial idyllic state of affairs is not going to last. Because Israelites were a good deal more prudish about the human body than we are, "naked and…not ashamed" could only be an unstable situation. So it is not surprising that this original condition in due course changes to one in which "they knew that they were naked" (3:7). Their first attempt at clothing is inadequate. In the end, the plot moves on to the normal clothed situation of present-day humanity, represented by "garments of skin" (3:21).

From Harmony to Alienation

The initially perfect relationship of delight and sexual bonding described in 2:23–24 eventually degenerates into a more realistic picture of human community that balances attraction and antagonism. Transgression leads to an increased distance between Woman and Man. God addresses Man and Woman separately and uses the second person singular to do so (3:9, 11, 13). Community dissolves into self-centeredness as they engage in finger pointing and use egocentric "I" language to defend themselves (3:10, 12–13).

Ultimately their relationship stabilizes into the ambiguous shape familiar to the reader, one affected negatively by pain in procreation and male domination in marriage (3:16). But there are positive elements as well. Man comes to recognize that Woman is not merely an object of his attraction derived from him (as one might conclude from 2:23–24), but the indispensable "mother of all living" (3:20). In the end, the author treats the two as "one flesh" still, but subordinates Woman's story into that of Man (3:17b-19, 22–24).

This movement from harmony to alienation also takes place in humanity's relationships with the ground, with the animals, and with God. Humanity and the ground begin in harmony, for Man is formed from the ground and put into a garden whose gorgeous, nourishing trees grow out of the ground (2:7, 9). At the close of the story, humanity is alienated from the ground as it brings forth frustrating thorns and thistles (3:17–18).

Humanity and the animals begin in harmony. Both are "living beings/creatures" formed from the ground (2:7, 19). Man names the animals. However, when we reach 3:15, humanity has become alienated from the animal world. There is reciprocal violence and hatred between Snake and Woman's offspring.

Most seriously, the relationship between humanity and God is damaged. In Genesis 2 God forms, plants, commands, and makes a partner, all for the benefit of Man and Woman. In contrast, in Genesis 3, God asks accusing questions and announces destructive consequences. For his part, Man distances himself from God with a classic denial of personal responsibility: "the woman whom you gave to be with me" (3:12). In the last scene, God acts to prevent humans, who are now "like God" to some degree, from getting any closer to achieving godlike status.

Harmony, intimacy, and integration have degenerated into disharmony, alienation, and disruption on all levels. Now life is full of ambiguity rather than harmony. We do till the ground and eventually return to it, but agriculture is a problematic way to make a living. We do marry, desire each other, and cling to each other so that life continues, but this is overshadowed by pain and male domination. Our relationship with God is damaged, but it nevertheless remains ambiguous rather than totally ruined, for God continues to act to benefit humanity: "God made garments" (3:21).

From Immaturity through Knowledge to Maturity

Humanity's initial innocent and unaware state is first suggested in 2:25 and is openly announced by Snake in 3:4. As we have already seen in chapter 2, an inability to recognize good and evil implies childishness and immaturity. The first readers would hardly have seen such naiveté as a virtue in adults who need to survive and succeed in the real world. Paradoxically, Woman and Man achieve a mature ability to perceive and judge only by violating God's command. We are never told why God sought to prevent humanity from attaining mature knowledge. However, the text takes it for granted that immortality must be denied to humans who have become "like God" in this way.

Permanent exclusion from utopian Eden pushes these newly aware, grown-up humans out into the real world. They go off into the world where the rest of the Genesis story takes place and the consequences of their disobedient choice play out—birth (4:1, 17, 25–26; 6:1), agricultural labor (4:2, 12; 9:20), death (4:8, 14–15, 23), and alienation from God (4:5, 16; 6:6–7; 11:6) and from other people (4:5–7, 9, 14, 23–24; 9:25–27; 11:7–8).

Separation and Reunion

Genesis 2–3 moves through a series of successive separations and distinctions. Man is separated from the ground. A river flows out of Eden, and four rivers split off from it. Two special trees are distinguished from the other trees. God forms animals from the ground. As Man gives them names, they are distinguished into types: cattle, birds, and animals of the field (2:20). Woman is surgically separated from Man. In the end, humans are permanently sent forth from the garden. However, reciprocal movements of return and reconnection also complicate the narrative. Woman and Man are unified as one flesh (2:24), leading to Woman bearing offspring (3:16) and to her role as mother (3:20). Woman moves toward her Man in desire (3:16). Humanity's original separation from the dust of the ground (2:7) turns out to be temporary, for in death we return to dust (3:19).

The Story as a Whole: From Then to Now.

Viewing the story of Eden as a whole and putting the various plot developments together, we can trace an overall movement from "then" to "now." Humanity's situation develops from an initial and exceptional sort of "pre-reality" into the disorderly and ambiguous reality that we humans experience today:

- From no cultivation of the ground to agriculture
- From solitude to community, sexuality, and procreation
- From Woman as an equal helper and partner to male domination
- From the unique reverse birth of Woman from anesthetized Man to the present painful process of reproduction
- From nakedness to socially approved and functional clothing
- From Snake with its crafty rhetoric to an on-going battle with real snakes
- From childlike ignorance to a kind of knowledge shared with God
- From childhood delights to an adult experience of work and pain, reproduction and death

Many human cultures have told similar stories of human origins. These exist for the purpose of orienting us in reality, showing us our "place in things." Such stories are told and retold because they satisfy our curiosity and answer our deepest questions about human existence. They are set into the primeval past ("in the day…God made the earth") because they describe the foundational realities of human existence. What happens for the first time in that unique primeval era also takes place over and over in our own time and in our own experience. In Eden the first human language develops. People fall in love for the first time. Humans make their first free choice and disobey God's command for the first time. Naïve children grow up into aware adults for the first time. Yet every human being in every generation has lived out and will live out those same experiences and events.

Is This a Tragic Story?

I have come to believe that the traditional notion of the fall of humanity focuses too narrowly on 2:15–17 and 3:1–19 to the exclusion of the rest of the narrative and fails to balance the negative consequences of the first human free choice with its positive ones.

At the end of the story, we humans are worse off in many ways. The farmer's life of toil and scarcity has replaced the gardener's life of ease and plenty. Frustrations and anguish abound (3:16–19). Loss of access to the tree of ongoing life is a tragic lost opportunity. But this is not the whole story.

It is hard not to be sympathetic with Woman (if not Man). Transgression is described as a free (but misguided) choice of knowledge over ignorance and of the fruit of a good-looking and appetizing tree. Snake takes advantage of Woman's immaturity and, ironically, of her current inability to "know good and evil." This choice leads to a wide range of consequences that sound much like the inevitable realities of adult life, with all its frustrations and complex, ambiguous interrelationships.

When the story is over, life is not completely tragic. Humans still live in a network of relationships with God and with each other. These are flawed relationships, but perhaps they are at least good enough. Assurances are implied in the negative consequences. The descendants of Snake and Woman are adversaries, but the positive side is that Woman will have offspring (3:15). The marital relationship has inequalities and afflictions; but there will be desire, and Woman will bring forth children (3:16). Humanity's relationship to the ground is cursed by frustrations and sweat, but God emphasizes three times that at least they will have something to eat: "you shall eat of it" (3:17), "you shall eat the plants" (3:18), "you shall eat bread" (3:19). Human toil ends in an appropriate return to the ground, our place of origin. Woman's new name, "Mother of All Living," indicates that the pangs, pains, and patriarchy of 3:16 are not the whole story and points to a future filled with life and procreation. Humans are estranged from God, but God remains engaged with humanity (3:21).

Eden is behind us, and the last words of the story emphasize that there is no point in yearning to return. We humans can still find meaning in our flawed human relationships and the promise of offspring, even though such meaning will be ambiguous and conditional. We have a vocation and a way of life outside the garden. We may be merely creatures in the sense that we experience pain, toil, death, and limitations; but we, nevertheless, remain God's creatures. We possess a capacity for perception, knowledge, and discernment that means we are "like God" in a limited way. Genesis 2–3 offers a reality check. The cherubim and whirling sword of flame mean that we cannot go back. To move on we must renounce Eden.

Growing Up in the Kindergarten of Eden

In Genesis 2, the two "babes in the wood" begin a process of maturation, awakening, and discovery. In Genesis 3, growing up leads to self-assertion, free choice, and confrontation with the grim realities of adult life. Woman and Man meet head-on with the fact of death and leave the kindergarten of Eden for life in the adult world. The early Christian teacher Theophilus of Antioch suggested that the problem in Eden was that adult knowledge came too soon to an immature pair and that God's prohibition had been intended to prevent this. The view that Eden describes humanity's maturation from innocent and ignorant childhood into sadder-but-wiser adulthood has become increasingly popular in recent years.

The strongest evidence for reading Genesis 2—3 though the lens of human maturation is 2:24, which describes a child's separation from parents and his or her eventual reintegration into society as an adult through marriage. As already mentioned, in Israel women, not men, left their family of origin to live with their mate's family. Therefore, this verse does not so much explain the customs of marriage as it does the process of growing up.

The whole Eden episode represents a movement away from childlike dependence within the garden to mature independence outside it. Man and Woman are separated from their parental God. The story refers to the entire scope of human life: birth (2:21—22; 3:16, 20), marriage (2:23—24; 3:16), an adult life of labor and pain (3:17—19), and its culmination in death (3:19). When the story is over, Man and Woman face life as adults. They no longer enjoy parental insulation from stark reality (a protected garden playground, nourishment without effort), nor do they live with childish illusions (unashamed nakedness, closed eyes, lack of awareness about good and evil). Their knowledge of good and evil is an awareness characteristic of functioning adults (see chapter 2). The pair can now engage with God in a defense and a shifting of blame, which, if not exactly "adult," still shows a growth in reasoning and language abilities. Hiding and self-defense show an understanding of adult responsibility. The consequences that result from their disobedience describe what grown-ups discover to be life in the real world: labor, frustration, sexuality, marriage, birth, pain, and death.

The Eden story also describes the discovery of sexuality and growth into adult sexual life. Humanity is created in two stages, emphasizing our sexual differences. When Woman is brought to Man, he responds with excitement. She is different and attractive. The author reminds us that sexual attraction is more powerful than parental attachment. Man seeks out Woman and clings to her. Woman desires man. When their "eyes are opened," they recognize problems inherent in nudity that young children do not see. They have developed a capacity to solve the nakedness problem as well as they could, given the inadequate materials on hand in a garden that included fig trees.

Let us revisit the Eden story in terms of the painful and wonderful process of growing up. Infantile Man lives alone in a glorious playground. He is faced with only one parental prohibition, a single "no-no." The emergence of animals gives him a chance to acquire language. As children often do, he starts with animal names: cow goes moo, piggy goes oink. When Woman appears on the scene, Man develops a more complex grammar, one that describes the relationship of one thing to another: woman taken from man. His language now even has two words for the same thing: ʾādām for man and ʾîš for male. Man's first sentence is also the first poem.

When Woman is brought to Man, he reacts in delight, like a boy discovering girls for the first time. He names himself no longer just Man (ʾādām) but now Male (ʾîš). His maleness has been "switched on" by the presence of Woman in a way that was not true before. Therefore, as humans grow up, their attachment to parents is eventually left behind; and new family arrangements are constructed (2:24).

They are naked; but as in the case of young children, this presents no problem. Children in the ancient world ran around naked for several years. Man and Woman know about their sexual differences (2:23), but these do not affect them in the way they would adults. Their lack of shame signifies an immature innocence about sexuality and an attitude of mutual openness. In a childlike way, each remains unconscious of the potentially judgmental gaze of the other. Shame is not yet part of their immature psychology. Shame signifies guilt or results from a lack of self-confidence and a feeling that one lacks what others have. These sorts of shame come with growing up.

Maturing children are confronted by new options, ambiguities, and questions. Education can be a subversive experience because learning new things can undermine certainties that children have inherited but not yet examined. Like a good teacher, Snake provokes critical thinking but never tells Woman what to do. She makes her own free choice to violate God's prohibition, based on her own independent perception. In one sense the cleverest animal outwits the still childish human; but in another sense, Woman takes a step toward independent adulthood.

Girls mature first. Is that one reason why Woman becomes the target for Snake's questioning? The author does not present her as wicked or arrogant, but as childish and too trusting. She craves what attracts her eye and sneaks a forbidden snack. Yet she is no longer simply a child. Woman evidences maturing judgment, mental development, and analytical thinking. She is aware not only of the tree's offer of good food and delight, but also of the benefits that wisdom would bring. Growing children seek to transcend the limits imposed on them. Woman is developing an independent self-identity. She leads the way for the somewhat less mature Man, who simply eats what he is given.

After their eyes have opened up, Man and Woman recognize that it is not appropriate to stay naked. Their new awareness is a consequence of their newly opened eyes. Self-consciousness means that they have matured to the point at which they can see themselves objectively, from the viewpoint of the other person. Now that they are growing up, naked bodies take on a sexual meaning, so they cover up their physical differences.

God interrogates Man and Woman, but not Snake. God treats them as responsible people who are capable of speaking for themselves and deserve a hearing. Concealment and self-defense show their maturing understanding of adult responsibility, even though at this point they are only trying to duck it. They have claimed their freedom to choose, but are not quite grown-up enough to take responsibility for their choice or its consequences.

Man does not simply confess, but defends himself. His defense may be inadequate and irresponsible, but at least it is factual in every respect. It sounds as though Man is claiming an adult prerogative to have his own perspective about the facts. Sure I ate, but you gave me Woman; and she gave me the fruit, so my responsibility is diminished. Woman's defense is also true and factual. She has reflected further upon Snake's words and now perceives them as trickery.

Adults like to indulge in nostalgia for a golden childhood like that described in Genesis 2, but most prefer being adults. Genesis 2–3 reminds us that growing up is inevitable and that we do not have the option of enjoying the naive, (supposedly) painless life of childhood. The course of our existence has been determined: adult knowledge, pain, frustration, and the shadow of death.

Step Eleven: Claims and Assertions

What claims or assertions does the text make about humanity and the world? What kind of God does it describe? What does this God do and care about? We read the Bible because we believe that it tells the truth about God and about us. The Eden story makes claims about humanity, God, and the relationship between humanity and God.

Genesis 2–3 explores the limitations and potentials of human existence. It is a pragmatic reality check on human claims to possess freedom, wisdom, and self-sufficiency.

First, we are curious creatures who seek out new knowledge and exercise our options to choose. We entertain questions and question authority. We experience aesthetic pleasure ("good for food…a delight to the eyes"). We suffer from vulnerability and fear, especially in the presence of God. Our reactions to God's scrutiny and our own self-knowledge are often misguided and inadequate (hiding, loincloths). We are absorbed by our work, but it remains frustrating. Yet, we are resilient and feisty, willing to carry on in the face of adversity.

Second, we do have free choice in at least some important matters. We can make independent decisions, including really bad ones. Even God's desire that the tree of knowledge remain off limits could not prevent Woman and Man from choosing to eat it. However, we exercise our free choice in a context that involves prohibitions, outside influences, and alternative perspectives. Because we have language skills, we are open to verbal seduction as Woman was. Because we live in community, we are vulnerable to peer pressure as Man was. We face limits to our free choice. Obviously, we cannot go back to Eden or achieve the godlike status that comes with immortality. In fact, even God's initial permission, "you may eat of the trees," really shows that we humans are not ultimately free and completely independent. If we needed God's permission to eat, then we were never really free to do whatever we wanted. In this sense, permission and prohibition are two sides of the same coin. Paradoxically, it was God's prohibition that created human choice, for only in the context of that prohibition did humans possess the possibility of a choice that made a meaningful difference. The final irony is that because humanity made its first free choice, an even more absolute limitation is now imposed upon us. The way back to the tree of life is blocked off.

Third, we humans are ultimately responsible for many negative aspects of human life. These things are not God's fault, and they are not a matter of "why do bad things happen to good people?" Eating from the tree was a disobedient act for which Man and Woman were properly held accountable. As a result of human self-assertion, we may be wiser and more mature, but in the process we have damaged the quality of human life.

Fourth, our relationships with each other, with the earth, and with God are damaged, but have not been destroyed. An imperfect network of relationships continues to function. Woman and Man continue to interconnect and collaborate (2:24; 3:20) even though their relationship is undercut by male domination (3:16). Humanity and the ground still have a reciprocal bond (3:23), although it is a troubled one and is overshadowed by death (3:17b-19). God still cares (3:21).

What is God like? What does God do and care about? To begin with, the God represented in this story is baffling and mysterious. God created the conditions that led to human disobedience and maturation. God put humanity into a garden with a forbidden tree placed conspicuously center stage and created a clever Snake to lurk in the wings. Was it not to be expected that forbidden fruit would arouse human curiosity and lead to disobedience? This is especially true when prohibitions are given without reason, for the absence of a rationale inevitably leads humans to consider alternative explanations.

We remain puzzled. Why would God seek to prevent us from acquiring mature knowledge? According to the Eden story, an unbridgeable gap separates human understanding and God's ways. God intends to prevent us from trying to be "like God" in any fundamental sense. However, although God's motives remain hidden from us, we are privileged to gain at least some insight into God's reflections (2:18; 3:22).

God is concerned with what is good for humanity (2:18), but also cares about the needs of the ground (2:5; 3:23). God is curious, seeking to discover how Man would name the animals (2:19). God is flexible, and so was willing to try another option when animals failed to work out as partners for Man. On the one hand, God seems willing to share the creative process with humanity, letting us give names (2:19, 23; 3:20) and procreate (3:15–16; 20). On the other hand, God carefully protects certain boundaries and refuses to let us push too far into divine prerogatives (3:22). God reacts to human defiance with consequences and limits (3:17–19, 23–24).

Ultimately, God remains in the right, and humanity has made the wrong choice. In spite of positive gains from our choice to eat, the overall mood remains one of sorrow and tragedy. Our relationship with God consists in large part of tragic collisions between our human potentials and God's command. The freedom and independence that seems so basic to our mature humanity has only been achieved through our infringement of God's good will for us.

Yet, God remains engaged with the human story. God incorporated our human penchant for making bad choices and our capacity for "knowing good and evil" into an ongoing future and prepared us for that future by making clothing. Perhaps even God's refusal to permit human immortality should be understood as a gracious act. Who could bear to live this life of suffering and frustration forever? Instead, we are permitted to die, and our return home to dust brings our misery to an end.

Our choice for autonomy and knowledge cannot be reversed. We cannot reverse the maturation process with all its frustration and pain and return to childhood. We have learned to think for ourselves and are stuck with the consequences.

Sources

In thinking about plot, I was inspired by Joel W. Rosenberg, "The Garden Story Forward and Backward: The Non-Narrative Dimension of Genesis 2–3," *Prooftexts* 1 (1981): 1–27. On the maturation theme, see Lyn M. Bechtel, "Genesis 2.4B-3.24: A Myth about Human Maturation," *JSOT* 67 (1995): 3–26, and Anthony York, "The Maturation Theme in the Adam and Eve Story," in *Go to the Land I Will Show You: Studies in Honor of Dwight W. Young*, ed. Joseph E. Coleson and Victor H. Matthews (Winona Lake, Ind.: Eisenbrauns, 1996), 393–410.

CHAPTER 4

Sibling Rivalry

Genesis 4:1–16

In this chapter, we will go through all of the interpretive tasks and questions listed in "Steps in Interpretation." (See the Introduction.) Remember to stop at the beginning of each subsection to come up with your own independent responses before going on to read my comments.

Step One: Bracket Off What You "Know"

Bracket off what you think you already "know" about the text; read with an open mind.

The greatest mystery in this story is why God accepted Abel's offering and not Cain's. One answer is to assume that Cain was just a wicked person with a bad attitude. This is certainly the impression one gets from the New Testament, which emphasizes Abel's supposedly contrasting righteousness (Mt. 23:35; 1 Jn. 3:12), even though Genesis itself says nothing about Abel's thoughts or behavior. Similarly, Hebrews 11:4 says that Abel's sacrifice was offered in faith, implying that Cain's was not.

The problem with any approach that charges Cain with wrong-doing before his sacrifice or a wrong attitude in regard to his sacrifice is that the text itself gives no warrant for this. Through a sort of interpretive sleight-of-hand, this common moralistic interpretation transfers Cain's attitude and behavior after his sacrifice to the time before it. In fact, God's reaction to Cain's resentment over the sacrifice incident is not to accuse him of a past or present crime, but to warn him to avoid falling into one (Gen. 4:7). Sin has not yet gotten him, but remains "lurking at the door." Cain still has the opportunity to fend it off. God does not even warn Cain to avoid doing evil, but rather admonishes him to positive action, to "do well" and to avoid not doing well.

"Am I my brother's keeper?" is the story's most famous quotation. Cain uses this rhetorical question to back up his defensive lie about his brother's whereabouts ("I do not know"). Am I responsible for my brother's fate? Am I someone who is always supposed to know where he is? After generations of pulpit exhortations, every modern reader knows the answer. Of course you are your brother's keeper, Cain! We are all responsible for our fellow members of the human family, who are all our brothers and sisters. But is that how the original readers would have responded?

The word for "keeper" is the problem. Nowhere does the Old Testament suggest that being our brother or sister's keeper is a social or moral obligation. People are keepers of animals and things. Shepherds are keepers of sheep. Man in 2:15 keeps the garden, and the cherubim in 3:24 keep (NRSV "guard") the tree of life. Only a bodyguard or a jailer would "keep" a person. Children may need keepers; but should mature adults, even brothers, have human keepers, minders, or babysitters? A keeper would know where Abel was at any moment, the way a shepherd knows where the sheep are or a zookeeper knows where the animals are. Only God should have this role (Num. 6:24; Ps. 121:4–5). Keepers are destructive to human autonomy, like certain patronizing and paternalistic social programs that undermine self-respect and interfere in people's freedom for "their own good."

No, the first readers would hardly have thought that Cain was under any obligation to be his brother's keeper. To them Cain's question would have sounded insolent and defensive, "I am not my brother's nursemaid, am I?" It might even imply a sarcastic remark directed at God: "In fact, aren't you supposed to be his keeper? After all, you accepted his offering and are obliged to protect him." But Cain's question would not open him up to moral condemnation for social insensitivity.

Step Two: What Is Familiar?

What is familiar about the text? How are we like the first readers?

Much about this story sounds familiar. Murder. Denial. Retribution. We know about family life and the struggle between siblings. We know that firstborn children tend to resent it when a second child comes along. We know that parents have favorites. Family life can be an arena for violent emotions—anger, jealousy, envy—and sometimes these lead to violence. We are not surprised that Cain cannot tolerate God's unexplained grace to his younger rival.

We know about specialized ways of making a living (only farmers and shepherds so far) and that rivalries between professions can create conflict. More serious yet is rivalry in the realm of religion. In this story, different ways of life lead to different religious practices: the farmer sacrifices crops; the shepherd offers meat. Religion becomes the starting place of violence, something we may consider ironic but hardly surprising.

We find Cain's sullen reaction perfectly understandable, especially because God has given him no reason for the disadvantage he has suffered. The Sermon on the Mount has taught us that anger is the precursor to murder (Mt. 5:21–22), which is virtually what God says to Cain in Genesis 4:7. We probably agree with God that good conduct ought to lead to happiness, not dejection, and that "a glad heart makes a cheerful countenance" (Prov. 15:13).

Genesis 4:11–12 describes the familiar problem of damaged soil failing to yield crops because of human mistakes.

We know about displaced persons who wander from one refugee camp to another and are often the targets of violence. We are also familiar with peoples who live a wandering, unsettled life because of their culture (the Romany people of Europe, the Khoisan people of Africa) or social misfortune (migrant farm workers, the homeless). The question as to whether Cain should suffer capital punishment for his crime (vv. 14–15) sounds particularly contemporary.

Step Three: What Is Unfamiliar?

What is unfamiliar? What surprises, puzzles, or shocks you? How are we different from the first readers?

How did Cain discover that God had ignored his offering? Perhaps we are supposed to assume that Abel became increasingly prosperous as a sign of God's favor, while Cain did not. It is likely, however, that this detail is passed over to prevent readers from focusing on that question or the issue of God's motivation. What is important is not

God's action, but Cain's reaction. It is also significant that God fails to explain to Cain why he has been treated differently, even in verses 6–7 where one might expect this. As in the case of God's prohibition of the tree of knowledge, a mystery without explanation leads to transgression.

Unexplained gaps in the plot are frustratingly common in the Old Testament. Written texts were rare and costly in the ancient world and would normally have been read aloud to an assembled audience. Sometimes those who read aloud must have behaved like performers or storytellers, using the written text as a basic guide, but adding details to flesh out the bare bones of the written script. Different storytellers could have filled in this narrative blank in different ways according to their own artistic creativity or inherited tradition: Abel became prosperous; Cain saw a bad omen; God appeared to Cain in a dream. In any case, the experienced interpreter soon learns that gaps in the plot are common and that there are often no answers to be had for some of the questions we have.

Much of the unfamiliarity we experience stems from our lack of cultural knowledge. For example, the author could assume that when Israelite readers encountered Cain (Hebrew *Qayin*), they would be reminded of their neighbors the Kenites (*Qeni*) whose name seemed to be derived from his. The Kenites were associates and allies of Israel with a nomadic lifestyle (Judg. 4:11). The Kenite connection means that Cain's destiny as a wanderer would have come as no surprise to early readers. This element in the story explained where the Kenites came from and why they had no settled home.

Cain and Abel seem to be in the social and legal situation of brothers who live together as part of their parents' household, before separating to form households of their own. Biblical laws and narratives reveal the jealousies and tensions that this situation could entail (Jacob and Esau in Gen. 25 and 27; Joseph and his brothers in Gen. 37; the laws of Deut. 21:15–17; 25:5–10; the prodigal son in Lk. 15).

The first readers would expect farmers and shepherds to sacrifice portions of their yield to God as a matter of course. The text offers us no particular reason to assume that this is the first time that Cain and Abel would have done this. Both grain and animal offerings were common in Israel, although Israelite readers would have noticed that these primal sacrifices lacked important elements of their own later religion—namely a priest, a holy place, and liturgical regulations. The author apparently did not feel any need to mention such obvious necessities as an altar and fire.

How can Abel's blood cry from the ground, and what sort of cry is this? Blood was momentous stuff in Israel. Blood represented life (Gen. 9:4), and the presence of blood signified violence (Deut. 21:1–9). The blood of violence spilled into the ground polluted it (Num. 35:33–34). Genesis 4:10 uses the Hebrew word for the cry of the victimized who are "yelling bloody murder." This is the cry with which an injured party would appeal for legal protection (Gen. 18:20; 2 Kings 8:3). It is the desperate plea of the hungry (Gen. 41.55), of the one who senses that death is imminent (Ex. 14.10), and of the rape victim (Deut. 22:24, 27). God says that Abel's blood is crying "to me," for in the Old Testament God was expected to heed such desperate cries for help (Deut. 15:9; 24:15; Isa. 19:20). No humans witnessed Cain's crime, but Abel's blood remains as a witness to it. Spilled blood cannot be hidden underground (Job 16:18; Isa. 26.21).

We moderns see reprisal killing as a sign of social breakdown and depravity and are not surprised that God would act to prevent it (Gen. 4:15). In contrast, the first readers would have evaluated properly executed vengeance against a murderer as a positive thing. Especially in earlier periods, Israelites could not rely on the government to deal with criminals. It was up to the family members of the victim to track down and execute the killer. Laws regulated this custom (Num. 35:16–21; Deut. 19:4–7), and 2 Samuel 14:5–11 provides a narrative description. God's protection of Cain by short-circuiting human retribution would have impressed the original reader as an exceptional act of favor. The author seems to assume that there are other people in the world beside the nuclear family of Adam and Eve who could threaten Cain.

We may take exception to the idea that Cain could "be hidden from [God's] face" and move "away from the presence of the LORD" (vv. 14, 16). However, sometimes the Old Testament indicates that whoever departs from the territory that the LORD governs enters lands where other gods rule (1 Sam. 26:19; Jon. 1:3).

Step Four: Key Words

What are the key words—words that are repeated or pivotal to the text's movement and meaning?

Knew in verse 1 is the well-known biblical expression for sexual intercourse. It recognizes that sex involves a personal recognition and intimacy that goes beyond the mere physical act. Cain's "I do not know" in verse 9 is the first real lie in Genesis and indicates further disintegration in humanity's relationship with God.

The story strongly emphasizes that Cain and Abel are *brothers*. The expression "his brother" is not really needed in verse 2, but is present to establish the theme. Genesis 4:8 reminds us again about the relationship—twice! Then the word is used four times in verses 8–11 to hammer home the status of Abel as Cain's brother. God seems to be pushing Cain to recognize this brotherly relationship. This constant repetition of brother accentuates the horror of Cain's crime and the revulsion we readers should feel about it.

As we have seen in Genesis 2–3, *ground* is an immensely important word in all these stories. Ground in the Old Testament is not just any terrain, but refers to the arable earth, the soil. Cain follows his father's example as a "tiller of the ground" (3:23; 4:2) and predictably brings his offering from the ground (4:3; Deut. 26:10). The ground is portrayed as though a living being, gulping Abel's blood down its throat (compare Num. 16:30, 32; Deut. 11:6), from which the blood screams out its cry as victim (Gen. 4:10–11). In Eden, humanity's relationship with the ground had been damaged, but only damaged (3:17–19). For Cain this relationship is completely destroyed. God did not curse Man and Woman, but Cain is cursed directly, cursed from the ground (4:11), estranged and separated from it. When he tills the ground, he will get no positive result (v. 12). Moreover, he is driven from the ground (v. 14; NRSV "soil"), that is, away from those regions where agriculture is possible. The corollary of Cain's alienation from farming the arable ground is that he must adopt the lifestyle of the world's nomadic peoples, wandering the earth (vv. 12, 14) and dwelling in the land of Wandering (Nod). Because he is alienated from the ground, it comes as no surprise that Cain builds a city and that his descendants develop ways of making a living other than settled agriculture (vv. 17, 20–22).

Repetition of *brought* and *offering* in verses 3–4 stresses that the source of Cain's resentment is God's dissimilar treatment of the two sacrifices.

In verses 5–6, Cain's *face* (NRSV "countenance") falls as a visible sign of the emotion he feels, and God reproves him for it. REB translates, "Why are you scowling?" The question of face returns forcefully as Cain is punished. In verses 14 and 16 he is driven from the "face of the ground" (NRSV "from the soil"), hidden from God's face, and departs from God's face (NRSV "presence").

The key word *kill* stresses the topics of murder and retribution. Israelite readers would have assumed that an "eye for an eye" reprisal was the appropriate payback for intentional murder (9:6). Consequently, Cain's positive future in 4:15 must have come as a shock to the first readers. Instead of the normally expected "anyone…may kill me," God surprises us with, "Whoever kills Cain will suffer a sevenfold vengeance."

Not all words pivotal to this story's meaning are repeated. Let us look at *field, sin,* and *mark.*

The crime takes place out in the *field* (v. 8), beyond the sight and hearing of witnesses. Second Samuel 14:6 reports a similar incident. In Deuteronomy 22:25–27, a woman caught having illicit sexual intercourse in the field (NRSV "open country") rather than in town receives the benefit of the doubt, the assumption being that out there no one would have heard her cry for help.

The word *sin* makes its first appearance in Genesis in 4:7. God warns Cain to control the potential for sin that his anger presents. This verse contains a vivid metaphor. Sin is a lurking, demonic creature poised to attack you, Cain. Like a carnivorous beast, it crouches at the door (of your heart?) ready to spring. It desires you, yet you can and must control it. Rather oddly, God's words here repeat much of the vocabulary of God's words to Woman in 3:16, in which God refers to Woman's desire for Man and his patriarchal rule over her. Here "desire" is a hostile, negative concept, and the verb translated "rule" in 3:16 is better understood as "master." This parallel vocabulary seems to invite the reader to compare Woman and Cain. Each made a wrong choice in the face of temptation.

The question of free will and the power to choose, central to the Eden story, returns to confront Cain. God does not seek to persuade Cain to avoid doing something wrong. Instead, God sets forth Cain's choice in positive terms, as one of either doing well or not doing well. Apparently, the point is not just to avoid murder. There is some right thing that Cain ought to be doing; but if he fails to do it, he will give sin the opportunity it seeks. The choice is completely up to Cain, who according to God is perfectly capable of dealing in a positive way with the rebuff of his sacrifice. Cain has not yet sinned, but is being admonished to do the right thing lest he fall victim to lurking sin. Verse 8 is Cain's response to God's warning. Cain does not choose to address God, but turns to speak to Abel instead. Like his mother and father, Cain fails the test.

God shows ongoing concern for Cain by providing a protective *mark* (v. 15). Cain's lament in verse 14 is accurate. Cut off from protection against the threat of reprisals on the part of his own family and from the safeguard of God's presence, Cain would be fair game for everyone. No human institution can protect this isolated fugitive, but God takes on the role of family protector and avenger. The sevenfold level of reprisal is high enough to discourage any assailant. By setting an explicit limit, God may also be seeking to prevent an uncontrolled cycle of revenge. To be effective, Cain's specially protected status has to be advertised in some visible way by a sign. We tend to imagine this as some sort of symbol or letter on Cain's forehead, but in some early Jewish traditions God gives Cain a set of animal horns!

Step Five: Opposites and Contrasts

What opposing or contrasting pairs of words or ideas are present?

Cain and Abel represent a sharp contrast. Cain continues the occupation of his father; Abel starts something new. The shepherd and the tiller of the ground represent the two most basic vocational options in the ancient world. The contrast in their vocations leads to a difference in their offerings: "fruit of the ground" over against "firstlings of [the] flock." They are also opposites in the sense of being elder brother and younger brother, with all the potential for conflict that entails.

However, an outside force, namely God, actually triggers their conflict. It would have been obvious to the first readers that farmers and shepherds would each bring offerings from their respective products. However, God's choice of one over the other shatters brotherly harmony. Why does God have regard for (pay attention to, notice, accept) one brother's sacrifice and not have regard for (disregard, ignore, overlook) that of the other? I have already suggested that it is pointless to try to blame any bad attitude or general wickedness on the part of Cain. Are we supposed to understand God's action as sheer divine free will, a capricious and inequitable choice of one of two equally appropriate and adequate sacrifices? Should Cain simply have resigned himself to God's arbitrary, inscrutable will? Certainly, the Bible represents God as free to choose whomever and whatever God wishes (compare Ex. 33:19). The terseness with which God's preference is described, without any explicit indication of motive, emphasizes God's sovereign freedom.

However, the text provides at least two reasons to think that the original audience would have expected that Abel's sacrifice would be more likely to meet with God's favor. First, Cain's gift was "of the fruit of the ground." However, because of what happened in Eden, the ground was now cursed (Gen. 3:17). So perhaps God did not accept

Cain's offering because it came from the cursed, miserly ground. Second, Abel's animal sacrifice was exactly the sort of offering that God was thought especially to enjoy. Even though offerings of grain and the like were part of Israel's sacrificial system, God was known for appreciating the fragrant smoke of sacrificed meat (Gen. 8:20–21; Ex. 29:18, 25, 41; Lev. 1:9). To stress that it was an offering of meat, Abel's sacrifice is described with double emphasis: "firstlings… their fat portions," that is to say, the best of the flock and their most delectable parts.

God disregards Cain's offering, but does that mean God has rejected Cain the person? To ignore is not to condemn. God has not written Cain off, for God gives him concerned advice, a fair warning, and a chance to show maturity and consideration for his brother. God seems to be telling Cain to accept the reality of his place in life. As long as you are a farmer of the stingy ground, you will never have the fatty abundance your brother enjoys. This is the reality of life outside Eden, and Cain must come to terms with it.

Step Six: Characters

What are the various characters like? What do they do? With whom does the text seem to encourage you to identify?

Eve announces that her motherhood unfolds in the context of her relationship with God. She is self-assertive: "I have produced." In fact, the verb she uses could even be translated as "create": "I together with the LORD have created a man." Perhaps these words reveal Eve's perspective on Man's earlier statements about her in 2:23 ("taken out of man") and 3:20 ("mother of all living"). She claims her role as mother with pride and proclaims that she has reversed the initial creative process of "woman from man" by bringing forth her own little man (*ʾîš*). She initiates the pattern "man out of woman" that will continue in 4:17–18, 20, 22, and 25.

Abel is an empty shell. He speaks no words. The report of his birth is curt compared to that of his brother, without any reference to intercourse and conception. Eve does not claim that she has obtained this second child "with the help of the LORD." I am reminded of how rarely parents get around to completing baby books for second children! His very name means "vapor," something ephemeral and transient. He is Mr. Nobody or Mr. Temporary. In contrast to Cain, the narrator does not even explain what his name means. Abel is secondary. He is described as Cain's brother seven times (vv. 2, 8, 9, 10, 11), but Cain is never described as his brother. His death is reported with no detail, no emotion, for this whole story is about the perpetrator of this crime, not its victim. Abel is remarkable for one thing only. The second born brings "firstlings" as a gift, and God has regard for his offering.

Cain is the center of attention. Eve expresses the joy that was proverbial at the arrival of one's firstborn (Jer. 20:15). Cain's emotional reaction to the sacrifice incident is described in verse 5, first from the inside ("angry"), then from the outside ("countenance fell"). Then Cain's reaction is revisited from God's perspective in verses 6–7. The text emphasizes that his act of murder is premeditated. He takes the initiative by addressing Abel (whatever he may have said; see the NRSV note to v. 8). The phrase "rose up against" indicates willfulness and intentionality. Cain tries to dodge his responsibility (much as his parents had) and distance himself from his relationship to his brother (v. 9). But he cannot, for in an ancient equivalent to modern forensic science, blood cries out from the ground. When confronted by his punishment, Cain laments to God in the manner of the psalms and gets a positive answer. Overall, Cain is an ambiguous figure. He is both condemned and protected, both a wanderer and a city builder (v. 17). Later generations were to remember him for the divine vengeance that shielded him (v. 24) and as an example of wickedness (Heb. 11:4; 1 Jn. 3:12; Jude 11). His story begins with an act of sacrifice to God, but he ends up even more distant from God and alienated from the ground than his parents were.

We must also think of *God* as a character in this story. God triggers the problem that Cain faces by valuing the two sacrifices differently, for whatever reason. God stays connected to Cain, initiating the dialogue with typical rhetorical questions (vv. 9, 10; compare 3:9, 11). God hears the cry of Abel's blood, but also gives heed to Cain's lament.

Two others players appear in this drama, *Abel's blood* and the *ground.* The blood cries out like a victim. The ground is described almost as a living entity, swallowing Abel's blood and reacting to it by withholding its strength from the murderer (vv. 11–12).

It is almost impossible to identify with Abel. Like the victim in a murder mystery, he seems to have been born and named merely to die. Cain is another story. We feel sympathy for Cain, who presents religious worship to God as we do, and then comes face to face with God's implacable mystery and ambiguity. It is also easy to identify with Cain's "justifiable" reaction to the unfairness of God's favoritism (up to a point, anyway). He is like the resentful elder brother in the story of the prodigal son (Lk. 15:25–32).

Step Seven: Patterns and Structures

What patterns give structure to the language and movement of the text? Look for repeated words or phrases. Look for "envelopes" or "bookends," concentric structures, and wordplays. Analyze how pronouns are used and how characters are addressed.

Analyzing the outline of Genesis 4:1–2 along with verses 17–22 and 25–26 shows that the basic shape of the chapter is one of a genealogy expanded into a story. That is to say, the story of Cain is set into the context of a seven-generation genealogy from the birth of Cain to the birth of Lamech's children. Cain is a main element throughout the chapter—as son, as murderer, as father and city builder, and finally as the reference point of Lamech's song.

Verses 1 and 25 surround the entire chapter with a framework. In each verse, Adam knows his wife; Eve gives birth, names her son, and explains the name in terms of God's action. There are *two* reversals in this pair of framing verses. The first has to do with who is named and who is not:

The *man* knew his wife *Eve* (v. 1)
Adam knew his *wife* (= "his woman") (v. 25)

The second reverses the primary actor and the secondary character involved:

I have produced…with the help of the LORD (v. 1)
God has appointed for *me* (v. 25)

The Cain and Abel story itself is structured primarily as a dialogue between God and Cain. A series of questions (vv. 6 and 7, two in v. 9, v. 10) structures the first part of this dialogue. Several other patterns increase reader interest. In verses 1–2 the names of the two brothers appear in a concentric pattern so that Cain surrounds Abel:

Eve bore *Cain*
she bore his brother *Abel*
Abel was a keeper of sheep
Cain a tiller of the ground.

This same concentric pattern is repeated in verses 3–5:

Cain brought
Abel…brought
The Lord had regard for *Abel*
For *Cain*…he had no regard

This structure seems to anticipate the action of Cain overpowering Abel.

Did you observe that in verse 6 God repeats exactly what the writer has just reported in verse 5? "Cain was...*angry,* and his *countenance fell*"..."Why are you *angry,* and why has your *countenance fallen?*" Each of these two "why" questions consists of three words in Hebrew. They draw our attention to the connection between inner emotion and its outer expression.

A striking repetition occurs in verse 8: "*Cain* said *to his brother Abel*" and, "*Cain* rose up *against his brother Abel.*" (Hebrew uses the same word for the preposition "to" and "against" here.) This reiteration accentuates the premeditated nature of Cain's crime and emphasizes the shocking circumstance that the victim was his brother.

A concentric pattern involving the last parts of verses 14 and 15 emphasizes the universal danger Cain would face and how perfectly God's protective mark will meet Cain's needs (author's translation):

> *anyone* who *finds* me
> may *kill* me...
> whoever *kills* Cain...
> *no one* who *found him*

We can often learn a lot about a text from the way it uses pronouns and the way characters are addressed. An analysis of pronouns in verse 1 uncovers Eve's pride and self-confidence as mother, with herself as the active "I" and God in the role of helper. In verse 4, the possessive pronoun is used to contrast Abel's sacrifice ("of *his* flock") with Cain's ("of the fruit"). Does this imply that Abel as shepherd had a greater feeling of ownership toward his offering?

Although God initiated the situation, the repeated second person pronouns in verses 6–7 emphasize that Cain alone was responsible for what he did. "If *you* do well...And if *you* do not do well,...its desire is for *you,* but *you* must master it." God's focus on Cain continues with the repeated use of "you" in God's announcement of punishment in verses 10–12: "what have *you* done?" "*your* hand," "when *you* till," "to *you*," "*you* will be." The reader cannot miss the message that this story is not about "Cain and Abel," but really only about Cain. Cain is the object of sin's desire, the one solely responsible for his own behavior, and the one who suffers the consequences of his crime. The repeated use of possessive pronouns with "brother" to refer to Abel underscores the horror of fratricide: "his brother" (vv. 2, 8);

"your brother," (vv. 9, 10, 11), and "my brother's" (v. 9). Cain's self-centeredness reveals itself in the emphatic first person pronouns in his famous line in verse 9: "*I* do not know. Am *I my* brother's keeper?" Cain's lament in verse 14 is also "me" focused.

Finally, did you notice that in verse 15 God shifts from addressing Cain as "you" to speaking about Cain in the third person? This communicates that these latter words are a "public announcement." They are not directed at Cain only, but are intended to have a universal impact on all who might encounter him.

Step Eight: Plot Movement

Describe the movement of the plot. How does it move from initial problem to resolution? Can you draw a flow chart or a diagram of this? What parts move the story forward, and what parts provide background or delay resolution?

The Cain story contains both action (vv. 3–5, 8, 15b-16) and dialogue (vv. 6–7, 9–15a), but the plot depends for its coherence on the dialogue between Cain and God. God initiates this dialogue (vv. 6 and 9), yet Cain does not speak to God until verse 9b. Both characters use the rhetoric of questions: Why? Where? Am I? What?

Introductory material in verses 1–2 and the conclusion of the plot in verse 16 bracket the story. Verses 1–2 provide exposition, introducing the characters (Cain, the LORD, and Abel) and their situation. Cain's journey away from the LORD in verse 16 marks the end of the story. Movement of a main character often indicates the beginning or end of a story unit (at the beginning: 9:18; 11:2; at the end: 3:24; 11:9). Speeches in verses 6–7 and verses 9–15 surround the murder in verse 8, which is the action center of the story.

The narrative begins by emphasizing the contrast between Cain and Abel: firstborn versus second born, potent name versus empty name, different professions, and contrasting offerings. The circumstances of their births and the different ways in which Eve reacts to their arrivals provide an early hint of impending discord.

Cain takes the active lead over his brother in bringing gifts. God's disregard of Cain's sacrifice (vv. 3–5a) leads to Cain's anger (vv. 5b-7), which in turn leads to murder (v. 8). But before the murder takes place, God's questions and warnings provide commentary on the meaning of what is about to take place and introduce a delay that piques reader interest. This murder will be the result of sin, but could have been avoided if Cain had resisted. Cain says nothing in response.

Following the murder, the first of two sets of speeches sounds like a trial, with interrogation and defense (v. 9), a witness (v. 10), and punishment (vv. 11–12). In verse 9, God asks Cain "where?" Like the "where?" question asked in 3:9, this inquiry invites the guilty party to acknowledge responsibility. Cain does not do so, but responds with a defensive, untruthful rhetorical question of his own (4:9). In verse 10 God comes back with a pointed question rather like that directed to Woman in 3:13. Indeed, God already knows where Abel is because his blood is crying out. God moves directly from question to accusation and sentencing, so that Cain is forced to remain silent.

The second set of speeches (vv. 13–15) represents Cain's lament and God's answer. The image of verse 13 is that the burden of Cain's lot in life is too heavy for him to carry. We do not know whether to translate "my punishment is greater than I can bear" (NRSV) or "my guilt is too great to forgive." In verse 14, Cain laments that God has driven him away, using the same verb that described the banishment of Man and Woman from Eden (3:24). Yet the consequences for Cain seem to be even worse, for God has driven him from the ground (soil) itself and even from God's presence. Cain laments in the style and language of the psalms. Psalms of lament seeking God's intervention and rescue often complain of being hidden from God's face (Ps. 13:1; 27:9; 44:24; 88:14) and threatened by hostile enemies (Ps. 41:5; 56:2; 59:1). Cain's exclusion from family and society and his wandering lifestyle will mean constant danger for him. Ironically, the murderer has discovered his own vulnerability to potential killers.

God responds positively to Cain's lament. God begins by saying either "not so" (NAB; NIV; NRSV) or "therefore" (NJB, see the NRSV note to v. 15.) *Not so* would seek to correct Cain's fear by declaring that he has misinterpreted the consequences of his expulsion. *Therefore* would concede that Cain's punishment is indeed harsh and so will be moderated. God's announcement does not explicitly identify the agent of this sevenfold retribution, but quite often the Bible uses the passive voice (here: "will suffer…vengeance") to indicate that God is the actor. Scholars call this the "divine passive" (compare "shall be hidden" in v. 14).

Parts of the story move it forward, while other elements pause to supply background or delay resolution. Verses 1–2a report initial events. Then verse 2b pauses to give background information about the two brothers. Action continues again in verses 3–5. Then God's warning in verses 6–7 interrupts to create tension and expectation on the part of readers: will Cain master sin, or will sin achieve its desire? This question is answered immediately by the events of verse 8. Now readers will be anxious to know how God will react to the murder. However, delay is again introduced by verses 9–10, exploring Cain's mind-set and the gravity of his crime. Only after verse 11 do the various consequences finally unfold.

Step Nine: Purpose and Intention

What is the text's purpose or intention or goal? What is it designed to do to you as a reader; how does it affect or change you?

Just as was the case with the Eden story, the Cain episode is concerned with explaining how features of present-day human life came into being. We learn where the wandering Kenite ("Cain-ite") people came from. Now there is a shepherd alongside the farmer. Human occupations begin to multiply, and conflicts between different lifestyles emerge. Family life begins to take a familiar shape, marked by parental favoritism and jealously between children. Religion makes its first appearance in the form of sacrificial gifts. Violence, bloodshed, and fear explode. Just as humans can join God in producing life (2:7; 3:20; 4:1–2), now they share in the divine prerogative over death. Without a doubt, life is sounding more and more like what we readers experience.

This story is bound to have a disturbing effect on us if we are willing to read it honestly and carefully. Friction between the human characters and God carries over from the Eden story and, if anything, gets worse. Human relationships are disfigured by deep ambiguity. Anger leads to murder, which leads to family estrangement, agricultural crisis, and the potential for unending revenge. Death enters human experience, surprisingly not as a direct outcome of God's warning in 2:17 or the disobedience of Woman and Man, but because of Cain's angry reaction to God's blatant act of preferring one sacrificial gift over another. Indeed, God turns out to be the most disturbing reality of all. By choosing the younger brother's gift, God may be demonstrating divine mystery and sovereignty, but also sets up the preconditions for Cain's crime. As was true with God's command about the tree of knowledge (2:17), mystery without explanation leads to transgression.

We readers are left with more questions than answers. Who was supposed to be Abel's keeper, really? God? Is it right that God should have favorites? Why does God violate expected standards by choosing the younger over the older brother? No wonder Cain had trouble handling all this!

Step Ten: Text in Context

How does context shape how you read the text and how does it contribute to its context?

Numerous contacts connect the story of Eden and Cain's story. They share a great deal of vocabulary: *till, know, keep, cursed.* The phrases "Eden in the east" in 2:8 and "east of Eden" in 4:16 build a unifying frame around the two narratives. Genesis 3:16 and 4:7 are strangely similar in wording. God confronts offenders with "where?" questions (3:9 and 4:9) and accusatory "what?" questions (3:13 and 4:10). Both stories follow a similar pattern:

- warning (2:16–17 and 4:6–7)
- misdeed (3:6 and 4:8)
- interrogation and trial (3:9–13 and 4:9–10)
- curse and consequences (3:14–19 and 4:11–12)
- continued divine connection and a mitigation of punishment (3:21 and 4:13–15)
- expulsion and alienation (3:23–24 and 4:16).

The theme of *ground* connects back to Eden and forward into stories that follow. Cain fulfills God's purpose for humanity by tilling the ground (2:5, 9; 3:23; 4:2). The curse on the ground in 3:17–19 is extended so that Cain himself is cursed with respect to the ground and driven from it (4:11–12, 14). This curse will eventually be modified or softened because of Noah (compare 5:29; 8:21–22; 9:20).

Genesis 2–3 is about knowing good and evil; Genesis 4 is about doing or not doing what is right. The move from Eden to Cain and Abel is not so much an intensification of human iniquity as an extension of it. Transgression emerges successively in the context of the two basic relational units of human existence, appearing first in the married couple and then in the nuclear family. Additional breakdowns in human relationships will emerge in the stories that follow.

Step Eleven: Claims and Assertions

What claims or assertions does the text make about humanity and the world? What kind of God does it describe? What does this God do and care about?

The story of Cain and Abel, like the story of Eden, is not just about the past. Rather it portrays a primal event with universal significance for the human race. It explores the issues of interpretation, human maturity, sin and its consequence, and God's nature.

First, like his mother in the previous story, Cain participates in the adventure of interpreting God's word in a developing situation. Like his parents, he is warned in advance of the dangers of transgression. Cain does not respond in words, so we are not informed as to how Cain interpreted or evaluated God's word of forewarning. However, his actions are response enough. In verse 8 Cain acts as though he has reinterpreted the meaning of "brother" as "rival," and in verse 9 defends himself against God's accusatory question with a perverse redefinition of "brother" as "keeper." Of course, a brother or sister is not a keeper in the sense of "warden" or "nursemaid"; but by offering this misinterpretation, Cain seeks to deny his legitimate brotherly responsibilities.

Second, the theme of maturity and growing into adulthood also carries over from Eden. Cain's story explores other aspects of maturity, namely sibling rivalry, emotional self-control, and anger management. Sibling rivalry is a natural part of growing up. A firstborn child displaced by a younger rival experiences it most sharply. Like Cain, children are dominated by their emotions; but adults need to learn ways to deal with them positively. In the end, Cain does what we all have to do. He leaves his father and mother behind and launches out into a new life to start a family with a spouse of his own (4:17) and, in so doing, fulfills the expectations of 2:24. This story also shows the maturation of human culture. Life is becoming increasingly complex. Differences in occupations can lead to inequalities and differing levels of success. Religion has also appeared in the form of sacrifice. New relationships are unfolding: mother and child, brother and brother, oppressor and victim, outlaw and avenger.

Third, this story explores sin and its consequences. According to Jewish and Muslim (Qur'an 2:30–37) tradition, the angels objected to Adam's creation because they predicted that humanity would introduce bloodshed into the world. This is exactly what Cain does. Like his parents, Cain has the freedom to choose the opposite of what God wants. Yet, God assumes that Cain still has the power to resist sin—even after what has traditionally been thought of as the fall of humanity. Actually, Cain's story sounds as much like a fall story as Genesis 2–3 does. Cain has free will to choose what to do, yet is also pressured by outside circumstances. Just as his mother succumbed to Snake's trickery, Cain fails to master the desire of lurking sin, which now appears unambiguously on the scene. Death also truly enters the world for the first time, as both murder and as potential retribution. The Eden event at least had some positive consequences, but Cain's ultimate situation is much graver. His parents were not directly cursed, but Cain is. For him, the life of the farmer will be fatally undermined by a total absence of crop yield and a wandering existence. Human misdeeds have a negative effect on the ground and lead to what today we would call ecological problems. Cain is alienated from earth and the nurture it offers.

Fourth, God continues to surprise us. Capital punishment for murder is a clear-cut expectation throughout the Old Testament. The one who kills is to be killed, often by a vendetta carried out by the victim's relatives. Moreover, as an outlaw, Cain would be a legitimate target for every stranger. In Cain's case, however, God chooses to block this expected and well-deserved penalty. God's benevolent response comes as a reply to Cain's fitting lament. Cain moves away from God's presence, but not from God's protection. God's protection takes the form of a threat of divine retribution. To our ears, the notion that God takes vengeance sounds completely negative and seems to run counter to what we assume about God's character. However, a cornerstone of Old Testament faith is that God is a just God, who defends the victims of wrongdoing and always strives to balance the scales of justice. Divine vengeance, for all its negative connotations, means that God seeks to inflict punishments that fit the crime.

Sources

My understanding of Cain's infamous question depends on Paul A. Riemann, "Am I My Brother's Keeper?" *Interpretation* 24 (1970): 482–91. I also used Kenneth M. Craig, "Questions Outside Eden (Genesis 4.1–16): Yahweh, Cain and Their Rhetorical Interchange," *JSOT* 89 (1999): 107–28, and Gunther Wittenberg, "Alienation and 'Emancipation' from the Earth: The Earth Story in Genesis 4" in *The Earth Story in Genesis* 2, ed. Norman Habel and Shirley Wurst (Sheffield: Sheffield Academic Press, 2000), 105–16.

CHAPTER 5

Vengeance Is Mine

Genesis 4:17–26

Step One: Bracket Off What You "Know"

This is not really a story in the normal sense of the word, but a genealogy (Gen. 4:17–22, 25–26) enriched by a poem (vv. 23–24). Most people are not familiar with these verses at all and are unlikely to have any biases or prejudgments about them. The one exception might be the notorious biblical riddle based on Genesis 4:17: Where did Cain get his wife? This question has led to all sorts of legends and theories. The usual answer is that she was an otherwise unmentioned daughter of Adam and Eve, from among those alluded to in 5:4. The narrator of this story just seems to take the existence of other people for granted (compare Cain's anxiety in v. 14), and pursuing this line of inquiry is a waste of time.

Step Two: What Is Familiar?

We are certainly familiar with the notion that social breakdown can go hand in hand with technological and cultural advances. The descendants of Cain are growing closer to our world. The division of labor is increasing, along with occupational specialization and diverse lifestyles. These developments make sense to us. We would expect that the demand for agricultural tools would create a need for metalworkers and that the development of more effective metal weapons would lead to increased violence. Swords and plowshares develop together. We also expect that music would be a part of our earliest human existence. This text neither condemns city life and technology nor praises them. This harmonizes with the modern attitude that technology generally represents progress, even though it also creates new and growing problems for us. Many of our culture's heroes are also inventors and innovators like Jabal and Tubal-cain.

These verses identify cities as foundational for human history. City life triggers splendid developments in human culture. We are likely to think of the Athens of Socrates or Leonardo da Vinci's Florence or Shakespeare's London. We know that originally cities were an outgrowth of the development of agriculture, so it is appropriate to conceive of Cain, originally a "tiller of the ground" (4:2), as the founder of the first one. Cities were made possible by the food surplus created by the agricultural revolution and made necessary to defend that surplus from enemies. The city was the core political unit of the ancient world. Whereas other contemporary cultures thought that the gods had a hand in the origin of cities, the Old Testament assigns this development to humans alone (4:17; 10:10–12; 11:1–9). The Bible's attitude toward the city, like ours, was mixed (positive in Isa. 1:26 and Zech. 8:3–5; negative in Isa. 1:21–23 and Mic. 3:9–12).

We are no strangers to the implacable brutality of Lamech's boastful song as he brags to his women about his strength and aggression. He threatens to go far beyond the practice of limited family vendetta to an exaggerated retribution of overkill. His song is a sort of psychological warfare intended to scare off adversaries, similar to Goliath's boast to David in 1 Samuel 17:44.

Other familiar features include the importance of family trees and genealogical data for establishing one's identity and place in society, giving family names to one's achievements (Gen. 4:17), and the notion of a "replacement child" to console a family for the premature death of a son or daughter (v. 25).

Step Three: What Is Unfamiliar?

We may be surprised to read of a close association between farmers and city people, but this was the norm in the world of the first readers. Most city dwellers went out to cultivate their fields each morning. In addition, ancient readers would have expected that metal smiths, musicians, and tent nomads would be linked together. These three groups were characterized by an itinerant life, although they would have been economically involved with city dwellers on a regular basis. Israelite readers may have been aware of the myths of other peoples that attached cultural developments and the origin of occupations to ancient celebrities. Possibly the information that Cain founded a city would have reminded readers that the usually nomadic Kenite people (hypothetically descended from him) had their own cities (1 Sam. 30:29).

Ancient peoples tended to conceive of social and cultural groups in terms of genealogical descent from a common ancestor. Thus the Edomites were purportedly descended from Esau (whose other name was Edom; Gen. 36), the Kenites from Cain, and the Canaanites from Canaan son of Ham (9:25). In a similar way, tent-dwelling livestock breeders, musicians, and metal smiths were thought to be descended from a single founding ancestor. The author ignores any notion that the flood would have meant that Jabal and Jubal and Tubal-cain could not really have been the biological ancestors of these groups. The point is that the cultural factors they introduced survived the flood and carried over to the present day.

We are probably uncomfortable with the notions of polygamy and revenge. The text, for its part, simply reports on Lamech's polygamy without evaluating it. It also assumes that the practice of vengeance is to be expected and expects the reader to know that proper retribution was limited in scope by custom and law (Num. 35 and Deut. 19).

In line with the ancient world's propensity for thinking in terms of genealogical pedigree, this text splits the world's population into two diverging families. Cain produces six generations of descendants culminating in Lamech. Seth fathers an alternate line of offspring leading down to Noah (4:25–26 + 5:3–31). If you compare these two genealogical catalogues, you may be puzzled to find that they share several pairs of similar or identical names. For example, there is an Enoch and a Lamech in each list (5:21–24 and 28–31).

Step Four: Key Words

The most striking of these is the step-up from *seven* to *seventy-seven*. The Israelite reader would have understood seven as representing comprehensiveness or completeness. Seventy-seven multiplies vengeance all out of proportion to what could ever be seen as reasonable or honorable. Jesus used a similar rhetorical boost in speaking of forgiveness, the opposite of retribution (Mt. 18:22).

Since this text is basically a genealogy, it unsurprisingly repeats vocabulary involving childbirth, ancestry, and naming: *knew, bore, wives.* In the NRSV, to be the *"father* of" refers to someone's place in a family tree (v. 18), while to be the *"ancestor* of" identifies the founder of a craft or lifestyle (vv. 20, 21; "Hebrew Word List"). The concept of *name* (as noun and verb) is clearly important, again as one would expect in a family tree. Cain names his city, Eve names her new little boy, and Seth names his son. The noun *name* is used to describe Lamech's wives and one son. In addition, the use of God's *name* becomes a new feature in religion in the days of Seth and Enosh. Here the reference is to God's special and personal name *Yahweh* (NRSV "the LORD").

Step Five: Opposites and Contrasts

We have already remarked on the step-up between *seven* and *seventy-seven,* which creates a contrast between *Cain* and *Lamech.* The similar sounding *Jabal* and *Jubal* also form a contrasting pair (vv. 20–21). Contrasting word pairs are typical in Hebrew poetry, and Lamech's boastful song contains two examples in verse 23. *Man* is contrasted with *young man* (literally "boy") and *wound* is intensified into *kill.*

In verse 25, *Cain* is the opposite of *Abel,* whom he slew, while *Seth* is the replacement for *Abel.* Parallelism between verses 17 and 25 creates a sharp contrast between Cain and his descendants on the one hand and Seth and his offspring on the other:

> *Cain* knew his wife and she…bore Enoch
> Adam knew his wife…and she bore…*Seth*

Step Six: Characters

Cain's history continues after his alienation from God's presence, the soil, and his family. Following the universal pattern set out in 2:24, he "leaves father and mother and clings to his wife." Cain has not been forgotten. His descendant Lamech indicates that the retribution associated with him has become proverbial (v. 24), and his mother remembers his crime (v. 25).

This *Enoch* is different from the better known Enoch descended from Seth, who "walked with God" (5:21–24). In Hebrew, the name Enoch fittingly means "Founder" or "Initiator." There are several other overlaps between Cain's descendants in 4:17–18 and the parallel list of Seth's offspring in Genesis 5:

- Irad and Jared (5:18–20)
- Mehujael and Mahalalel (5:15–17)
- Methushael and Methuselah (5:25–27)
- Lamech and Lamech the father of Noah (5:28–30)

This is in addition to Kenan (*Qenan*) in 5:12–14, whose name is similar to Cain (*Qayin*).

It seems clear that similar names from a common pool of traditions concerning pre-flood worthies have been preserved in two different orders in two different lists. These lists seem to have been included to bridge the time between creation and flood, to allow time for the earth's population to increase (6:1), and to contrast the negative line of Cain that ends in Lamech's violence with the positive line of Seth that leads to Noah.

Adah ("Ornament") and *Zillah* play out roles for women typical in a patriarchal society. They are mothers and serve as an audience for their husband's arrogant boasting. Zillah's daughter *Naamah* ("Pleasant") fills out a pattern of two children for each mother, but does nothing else.

The names *Jabal* and *Jubal* form wordplay (like Tweedledum and Tweedledee). Appropriately enough, Jubal sounds like the Hebrew word for ram's horn trumpet (from which the English word "jubilee" comes). The first part of *Tubal-cain* echoes the sound of Jabal and Jubal, and the second part duplicates Cain's name. Abel had been the first keeper of sheep and goats; Jabal begins keeping larger cattle and initiates the transient lifestyle of dwelling permanently in tents (like the Kenites and Midianites, Judg. 5:24; 6:5). Ancient smiths and musicians often lived a nomadic existence as well, as they do in some areas of Africa and the Middle East today.

Lamech and his offspring are the last in Cain's line. His violent nature reiterates and even exceeds that of his ancestor and points forward to the conditions that will make the flood necessary (Gen. 6:5, 11).

After their family tragedy, Adam and Eve begin life again by producing another son. *Seth* and his son *Enosh* represent the opposite of what Cain's family line stands for. Unlike Cain, who has been driven from the LORD's presence, Seth marks the time when people call on God's special name "Yahweh." The text encourages the reader to identify with Seth and Seth's line. Who would want to be descended from the first murderer and brutal, boastful Lamech? Moreover, the name of Seth's son Enosh means "human being" and suggests a fresh start and a more direct connection to us.

Step Seven: Patterns and Structures

If you made a diagram or chart of these verses, you probably noticed that for the most part they form a genealogy or family line. This genealogy continues what was begun in 4:1–2. The first six generations (vv. 1–2, 17–18) consist of a simple, direct line from father to son, with side references to various cultural advances. Verses 1–2 allude to two professions. Verse 17 adds that of city builder. Generations three through six are reported by verse 18. Lamech is father of the seventh generation, at which point the linear genealogy breaks out into a tree (vv. 19–22), describing his two wives and four children. In this seventh generation, three new occupations are inaugurated.

Verses 25–26 start the genealogical progression over again, going back to Adam and Eve and tracing the second segment of their line. The word *again* in verse 25 makes this connection clear. Seth and Enosh make up a two-generation genealogy, and again there is an advance in culture, this time having to do with religion.

Verses 17–18 and 25–26 form a pleasing, artistic frame or envelope around the genealogies of Cain and Seth:

Cain knew his wife and she…bore Enoch
> A   He built a city and named it…after his son
> B   to Enoch was born Irad
Adam knew his wife…and she bore…Seth
> B'   to Seth…a son was born
> A'   People began to invoke the name of the Lord.

The language of verse 25 parallels that of verse 1 even more closely, creating a framework that encloses the entire chapter. In each of these sentences, Eve bears and names a son and, in so doing, recognizes God's role in his birth with a significant wordplay (see the NRSV footnotes). Literally, Eve calls Seth another "seed" (NRSV "child"), indicating that the reality God predicted in 3:15 is coming to pass. "Another seed" implies not just a single child, but also a second, separate lineage, a whole line of descent in contrast to the line of Cain. Did you notice that Eve names her babies (4:1, 25), but Seth names his son? If you read ahead into Genesis 5, you will see that 5:3 disagrees with 4:25 concerning who named Seth.

Eve is not identified by name in verse 25, only designated as Adam's wife. The reverse is true in verse 1, where Adam's name does not appear but Eve's name does. At the same time, Eve makes herself the principal actor in verse 1 while giving God the leading role in verse 25.

The *man* knew his wife Eve…
  "*I* have produced" (v. 1)
Adam knew his wife again…
  "*God* has appointed for *me*" (v. 25)

These sorts of exchanges and reversals are typical of framing verses in Old Testament stories. By keeping alert to these envelope constructions, the interpreter can ascertain what materials the ancient writers wished to have readers consider together. Taken together, verses 1, 17, and 25 should be understood as instructions to the reader: Think about the genealogies of Cain and Seth as contrasting parallels, and at the same time consider them in connection with Cain's act of murder.

Israelite readers would have recognized Lamech's poem as a boasting song, similar to that of Samson (Judg. 15:16) and the adulation offered David (1 Sam. 18:7). Lamech is bragging to a captive audience made up of his wives. His song reflects the shapes and patterns of Hebrew poetry. There are three parallel couplets (two line units): verses 23a, 23b, and 24. Let us investigate how the parallelism works.

In verse 23a, Lamech begins with an introductory address to his audience, similar to what one finds in Exodus 15:21 and Psalm 34:11. This address functions as a call to attention, alerting hearers (and readers) that something significant is about to follow. The parallelism of the first couplet (v. 23a) is fairly obvious: "Adah and Zillah" is the equivalent of "you wives of Lamech," and "hear my voice" is paralleled by "listen to what I say."

The second couplet (v. 23b) describes Lamech's unrestrained vengeance with the parallelism of intensification: first one bad thing and then something even worse. He responds to a mere wound or blow by killing the offender. He slays not only a grown man (which is bad enough), but even a mere youngster (which is worse). The Hebrew word translated "young man" is really "boy," perhaps indicating a young, upstart warrior.

This pattern of intensification recurs in the third couplet (v. 24). The sevenfold standard set up for Cain is not good enough for Lamech—he intends to retaliate at a level that is eleven times more intense. The normal poetic step-up from "seven" would be "eight" (compare Eccl. 11:2 and Mic. 5:5), but Lamech goes beyond all bounds. Both "avenged" and "seven" link this verse back to Genesis 4:15, where these words also occur.

English translations usually put Lamech's words into past tense. Understood this way, he is boasting about his record. "I have already behaved in this way, so watch out, enemies! I have already demonstrated a ferocity and strength beyond any provocation you may offer!" However, it is also possible to translate these verbs in such a way that they assert Lamech's present and future willingness to act with unrestrained intensity:

> I would kill a man to avenge a mere wound,
> I would kill a mere boy to avenge a blow.
> If Cain is avenged seven times
> Then Lamech will be seventy-seven times.

Lamech would then be saying, "This is my potential and capacity for vengeance. Be warned!"

Perhaps this little poem originated in some ethnic community that conceived of Lamech as its founding ancestor and which preserved and passed it on as a sort of group slogan. As such, it would be similar to the belligerent tribal sayings found in Genesis 49:17, 19, 23–24, 27 and Deuteronomy 33:17, 20, 22.

The bottom line is clearly that unrestrained human retribution is not a good thing. It characterized the low moral state into which humanity had fallen, or at least that portion descended from Cain.

Investigating pronouns often provides useful clues for interpretation. Did you notice the shift between verses 23 and 24 in Lamech's song? He begins by speaking about himself in the first person ("my…I…I…me…me"), but then shifts to the third ("Lamech") to give a general warning to any who might threaten him. This is the same pattern that we noticed in 4:10–12, 15, where God first speaks directly to Cain as "you" and then shifts to announce a public warning of reprisal using Cain's name. If we widen the focus to the entire chapter, we can see that the contrast between the use of pronouns in verses 1 and 25 seems to indicate that Eve's attitude has changed to become less assertive. Verse 1 says, "I have produced…with the help of the LORD," but verse 25 changes to, "God has appointed for me…"

Step Eight: Plot Movement

A shared genealogical skeleton (vv. 1, 17–22, 25–26) integrates the contrasting family lines of Cain and Seth with the story of Cain and Abel. This genealogy moves from father to son in verses 1, 17–18, 25–26, but branches out in verses 19–22 to consider Lamech's children and to provide a setting for his song. The whole of Genesis 4 is also held together by repeated references to Cain (vv. 17, 22 [Tubal-cain], 24, 25) and by the topic of violence and vengeance.

Two complementary movements drive the plot. First, the story of the birth and occupational divergence of Cain's descendants leads to a boastful song of violent retribution (vv. 17–24). This echoes the previous story, in which Cain's birth and his occupational difference from Abel descended into murderous violence and the prospect of revenge (vv. 1–16). Both plot lines point forward to the degeneracy that leads to the flood.

Second, the words *again* and *another* in verse 25 hold the contrasting family lines of Cain and Seth together and instruct the reader to compare them. The pointed reminder in that same verse that "Cain killed" also invites us to compare Cain and Seth. Comparison is again provoked by the similarity in names between Cain's line and those of Seth's line in 5:6–31. When we compare the two genealogical lines, it is clear that the one from Cain to Lamech is presented negatively, while the one beginning with Seth and Enosh and leading to Noah is evaluated positively.

Step Nine: Purpose and Intention

As with the Eden narrative or the Cain and Abel episode, the early stories in Genesis display an interest in explaining how things got started. They are etiologies that account for present realities by recounting stories of origin. This text tells us how cities, occupations, and cultural achievements got their start.

The flood does not rupture humanity's cultural history, which simply carries over into the world of today. We are told that city life and its accompanying technological and artistic advances were human achievements, not gifts the gods bestowed on humanity. Perhaps this text intends to throw a negative light on urban civilization by assigning it to Cain's family.

At the same time, verse 26 describes the origin of something unambiguously positive, namely the use of God's special name Yahweh in worship. It is not completely clear whether "at that time" specifically indicates the time of Enosh or whether the entire primeval era is intended. Because verse 26 comes last in this textual unit (before the obvious new start of "this is the list" in 5:1), it has an especially strong impact on the reader. Scholars call the emphasis given to the last words of a text "end stress." This last verse conveys that the religious use of God's personal name Yahweh is something so fundamental to human existence that it was used long before Israel itself appeared on the scene. This emphasis is different from that of other texts that trace the use of the name Yahweh to the time of Moses (Ex. 3:14; 6:3).

Step Ten: Text in Context

We have already described how these verses continue the topics of occupational diversity, violence, and vengeance the Cain and Abel story introduced. The story of Cain's descendants fits equally well into the context of Genesis 2–11 as a whole. Like all these stories, it describes the continued unfolding and structuring of human life. The language of beginnings in 4:26 ("began to invoke") will be repeated in upcoming stories: 6:1, "began to multiply"; 9:20, "first to plant"; 11:6, "the beginning of what they will do." This section starts a saga of human population growth that will find its first culmination in the story told in 6:1–4. Lamech's violence sounds like the first installment on the evil inclination of the human heart that will lead to the flood (6:5). In the Babel story the topic of city building will return, along with the notion that city-based civilization can distance humanity from God's purposes.

Step Eleven: Claims and Assertions

Much of this text implies a negative judgment on humanity. The non-agricultural focus of Cain's lineage (cattle and tents, music and metallurgy) seems to represent a detour from God's intention that humans are intended to till the ground (2:15; 3:23). Cain's violence and the path of retributive vengeance are multiplied (literally) in Lamech's song.

However, positive elements also emerge. If we remember Genesis 1:28, we will understand that this first surge of human population growth comes in obedience to God's command, "Be fruitful and multiply" (1:28). This story asserts that the (mixed) blessings of city life, technology, and the musical arts are strictly human achievements. They are not gifts from the gods, nor were they stolen from them (in contrast to the Greek story of Prometheus, for example). Perhaps progress and urbanization are not totally negative developments, but so far they have originated only with Cain's family line.

According to Eve, God still remains closely engaged with the human story in spite of the wrong turn Cain's line took. This is evidenced by God's active role in the birth of Seth, "another *seed*" (v. 25). Verse 26 claims that the use of God's proper name Yahweh is vital to effective worship. Abraham will provide early examples of this practice in Genesis 12:8 and 13:4. Israel considered its ability to call on God using God's own special name as a gracious divine gift (Ex. 3:13–15).

Sources

My understanding of Lamech's song relies on Patrick D. Miller Jr., "*Yeled* in the Song of Lamech," *Journal of Biblical Literature* 85 (1966): 477–78, and Stanley Gevirtz, "Lamech's Song to His Wives," in *"I Studied Inscriptions before the Flood": Ancient Near Eastern, Literary, and Linguistic Approaches to Genesis 1–11,* ed. Richard S. Hess and David Toshio Tsumura (Winona Lake, Ind.: Eisenbrauns, 1994), 405–15.

CHAPTER 6

Boundary Violations and Evil Hearts
Genesis 6:1–8

Step One: Bracket Off What You "Know"

The first part of this text has probably created more puzzlement than any other in the book of Genesis. Who are these "sons of God" supposed to be, and why are they involved with human women? Some early Christian interpreters took them to be males descended from Seth who married the daughters of Cain (Augustine). However, the usual tendency has been to consider them as "fallen angels." In early Judaism, this text became the basis for an extremely popular "fall story" that told of the revolt of certain angels against God and their sexual involvement with humans. This idea was also popular in Christian circles, as witnessed by 2 Peter 2:4 and Jude 6. However, as we shall see, Israelite readers would not have been particularly mystified by this reference to the sons of God and would not have considered them to be fallen angels.

Those who read this story without paying careful attention tend to take it for granted that these human women were the objects of brute lust on the part of their superhuman sex partners and that marriage was forced upon them. However, we should not automatically assume this. The verb *take* with the object *wives* does not necessarily imply coercion. Rather this is the normal way to describe marriage in the Old Testament (for example, Gen. 4:19). As far as "brute lust" is concerned, Jacob's love match with Rachel also begins with the episode of seeing a beautiful woman (Gen. 29:10), as does Samson's acquisition of a Philistine wife (Judg. 14:1–2; "he saw a Philistine woman…take her for me" [NRSV "get her"]). The sequence—(1) positive evaluation of a woman, (2) taking in marriage, and (3) bearing children—represents the normal progression of an Old Testament marriage.

However, given the difference in status and power, the author may have intended to describe some degree of compulsion in what the sons of God did. This is the case with Pharaoh and Sarah (Gen. 12:14–15; "saw her…the woman was taken") and probably with David and Bathsheba (2 Sam. 11:2, 4; "saw from the roof a woman…sent messengers to take her" [NRSV "get her"]). The sons of God are active and get what they want (saw, took, chose, went in to). The human women merely carry out the natural outcomes of these male actions ("bore children").

The interpreter should bracket out any premature judgment that this is a story about sin and punishment. The text does not criticize the actions of the sons of God, and the humans involved certainly do nothing for which they could be blamed. No punishment is imposed on the sons of God, even though they have violated the boundary between the divine and the human. God's decision only affects the innocent humans. This life span restriction is applied universally to the whole of humanity ("mortals…for they are flesh"). It is not limited just to the children of these mixed marriages. Moreover, it really sounds more like a precaution than a punishment.

It seems obvious to modern interpreters that the 120 years of Genesis 6:3 refers to a limit on the human lifespan. However, Augustine, Jerome, and Luther thought of these years as a period of gracious concession granted because of fleshly weakness. Only after this 120-year period would God withdraw this life-giving spirit and send the flood.

Step Two: What Is Familiar?

Even though this story is bizarre in many ways, a few familiar elements pop up. Population increase is an ominous feature of modern life. We certainly understand the power of beauty and sexual attraction. We remember our own war heroes from bygone times.

That human hearts are "only evil continually" (v. 5) is no surprise to us, who have been taught that "all have sinned and fall short of the glory of God" (Rom. 3:23). However, it would have come as quite a shock to the first readers. The Old Testament rarely emphasizes human depravity, but instead assumes that people have the ability to obey God's law and are perfectly capable of doing the right thing if they choose to do so (Deut. 30:11–14).

Step Three: What Is Unfamiliar?

Who are these "sons of God"? The first readers would not have been particularly mystified by this reference. In the ancient worldview, God was seen as ruling like a human king, seated on a throne surrounded by superhuman courtiers and subordinates standing ready to do God's bidding. This scene is vividly described in 1 Kings 22:19–22 and Isaiah 6:1–8. The book of Job begins in God's throne room (Job 1:6; 2:1), and those assembled are called "sons of God" (NJB; NAB; NRSV "heavenly beings," but see the footnotes). These "sons of gods" sing God's praises in Psalm 29:1 and at the dawn of creation in Job 38:7. In Psalm 89:6 the LORD is proclaimed as incomparably more powerful that they are. In Hebrew idiom, "sons of" is a way of saying "belonging to the category of." The "sons of the prophets" were members of a prophetic group (1 Kings 20:35). Thus the "sons of God" are those who belong to the category of divine or godlike beings. God addresses these "junior grade gods" as "us" in Genesis 3:22 and 11:7.

The authors and readers of the earlier portions of the Old Testament were not exactly monotheists in anything like the later Jewish, Christian, and Muslim sense. In Psalm 82, Israel's God judges and condemns other gods in the midst of the divine council, the assembly of the gods. Deuteronomy 32:8–9 (NRSV) describes how the nations were once parceled out to their national gods.

Sex between heavenly beings and humans would not have been completely unexpected to ancient readers. They would likely have been familiar with stories of half-divine, half-human heroes like the Babylonian Gilgamesh. We ourselves may remember myths about Greek gods having sex with humans and producing heroes like Hercules. Israelite readers, however, would still probably have been shocked by the idea of intermarriage between the sons of God and human women. It was supremely important that the boundary between even junior-grade divinities and humans remain inviolable. We have already seen how God expressed the importance of keeping this barrier intact when the human pair was driven from Eden (3:22–24).

Creation meant setting up divisions and boundaries. Heavenly bodies belong in the sky, plants and animals on the earth, fish in the waters (Genesis 1). God created the various plants and animals "according to their kinds" (1:11, 12, 21, 24, 25; RSV). Therefore it was vital that entities always remain in their proper places and that categories not be mixed up. For this reason the Old Testament has laws about keeping things separate. Each gender must wear its own clothing style (Deut. 22:5). Don't sow different kinds of seed in your field or plow with mismatched animal species (Deut. 22:9–10). Fish without scales aren't "fishy" enough and are forbidden as food (Lev. 11:10–12). The same is true of domestic beasts that fail to match the proper pattern for such animals, that is, divided hoof and chewed cud (Lev. 11:4–8). If different species of animals were not to be bred together (Lev. 19:19; compare 18:23), how much more should this be true for deities and humans? Any mixing of what was godlike and what was human through sexual relationships would be something worthy of a response as catastrophic as the flood.

We are likely to be surprised that the human life span is as long as 120 years. In the world of the Old Testament, however, this represents the upper limit of the great heroes of Israel. Joseph and Joshua died at 110; Moses at 120.

The idea that God could feel sadness and be sorry for a previous action may sound strange. We tend to think of God as unchanging, as One who has designed a fixed plan for the universe and knows the future in all its details. These common notions are due to the pervasive influence of Greek philosophy on Western thought. In contrast, the God of the Old Testament is engaged with the world and reacts to human decisions and behavior. According to Jonah 3:10, God changed a predetermined plan to destroy Nineveh because they repented: "When God saw...God changed his mind" (using the same verb translated as "be sorry" in Gen. 6:6). This parallels Genesis 6:5–6– "The LORD saw...and the LORD was sorry"–but in Genesis the result is destruction rather than deliverance.

Again, unlike the God inherited from philosophy, the biblical God has a rich emotional life, and Old Testament texts are sometimes willing to penetrate into God's psychology (Jer. 12:7–13; Hos. 11:8–9). As One who is deeply involved with irresponsible humanity, God loves, God becomes angry, and God can be "grieved...to his heart" (Gen. 6:6). God suffers when faced with the need to punish, feeling sorry that he had created humanity.

Step Four: Key Words

Verses 1–7 are held together by eight occurrences of *'ādām* (humankind or human being), although the NRSV obscures this. The entry "man in the generic sense (*'ādām*)" in the "Hebrew Word List" shows that the NRSV uses a variety of equivalents to render this single Hebrew word: "people," "mortals," "humans," "humankind," and "human beings." This results from the translators' desire to use gender-neutral language. This otherwise admirable practice creates more distance from the Hebrew original for the interpreter who is restricted to English. I suggest using the older RSV to check when you suspect that NRSV is paraphrasing to avoid linguistic sexism.

Thus the key word *'ādām*, humankind, holds these verses together and reveals their central topic:

v. 1 humankind began to multiply
v. 2 the daughters of humankind were fair
v. 3 shall not abide in humankind forever
v. 4 went into the daughters of humankind
v. 5 the wickedness of humankind was great
v. 6 sorry that he had made humankind
v. 7 blot out humankind...humankind and beast

Up until now, *'ādām* has referred to the first male human being, either as a common noun or a proper name. Here for first time *'ādām* means humanity in general. This usage points forward to the story of Babel, which also concerns the early situation of the whole human race (11:5).

Face of the ground (vv. 1 and 7; NRSV "from the earth" in v. 7) links this story back to the punishment of Cain, who was banished from the face of the ground (4:14, NRSV "from the soil") and forward to the Babel story, which deals with humanity's further dispersal over the face of the *earth* (11:8–9).

These *daughters* (v. 1) are more specifically *daughters of 'ādām* (vv. 2 and 4), that is, human women. *Daughters of 'ādām* creates a pointed contrast to the their divine sex partners, the *sons of God*. The progress of fertility and multiplication goes on as these women *are born* (v. 1) and then *bear* in their turn (v. 4). However, God's reaction in verse 3 makes it clear that something has gone wrong.

The *earth* in the sense of planet Earth (and thus not heaven) is the setting for this drama of intermarriage and divine reaction (vv. 4, 5, 6): the Nephilim are *on* it, human wickedness was great *in* it, and God is sorry about having created humans *on* it.

The writer emphasizes God's change of heart by repeating the verb *sorry*: "the LORD was sorry that he had made"; "I am sorry that I have made" (vv. 6–7).

Other words are not repeated but are still important. *Began* in verse 1 reminds us that we are still in the mythic story world of primeval first things, when people began to invoke God's name (4:26), plant vineyards (9:20), go to war (10:8), and engage in other initial ventures with future implications (11:6; the same Hebrew verb is used in all these verses). This story is about prehistory, the time "of old" (6:4). "Began to multiply" sounds as though this story is meant to be taken as a flashback to the genealogical expansion of Genesis 4 and 5.

Fair translates the Hebrew word normally rendered as "good." "Saw that they were *good;* and they took" sounds like an ironic parallel to Woman's earlier perception of the tree: "Woman saw that the tree was good...she took" (3:6). Once again, perception leads to desire, and desire leads to a dangerous choice (compare "they chose"; 6:2). Early readers would have known of other stories that began with a perception of womanly beauty leading to destructive consequences. We have already referred to the dangerous beauty of Sarah (Gen. 12:10–20) and Bathsheba (2 Sam. 11:2, 4). Beauty was also the catalyst of the Tamar tragedy (2 Sam. 13:1–19) and plays a role in the more ambiguous tale of Abigail (1 Sam. 25:3, 39–40).

Nephilim means "fallen ones." Are they termed "fallen" because they have fallen from heaven to earth? The text says nothing about this. Or are they fallen in the sense of being dead heroes of the past, fallen in battle? Ezekiel 32:20–21, 27 speaks of those fallen in battle who go down to the world of the dead as warrior heroes. The Nephilim existed "in those days," in the mythic past, but "also afterward," apparently a reference to the terrifying Nephilim encountered by Israel when they invaded Canaan (Num. 13:33). Perhaps they are to be identified with the indisputably human warriors mentioned in the last part of verse 4, who are "of old," that is, figures from Israel's epic past.

The word *inclination* (v. 5) comes from the same root as the verb "to form, shape" used in 2:7, 8, and 19. It is the first element in a three-part chain: "*inclination* of the *thoughts* [plans, intentions] of their *hearts.*" *Inclination* used with *heart* indicates the nature and purposes of the human mind, its proclivity to pursue predictable and typical intentions. We might say that the *design* of the human heart leads predictably to its *designs*. Humanity's plans and choices are now seriously bent into a direction favorable to wicked and harmful choices. "We have followed too much the devices and desires of our own hearts" (*Book of Common Prayer* [New York: Seabury Press, 1979], 41).

In the context of what we have read about Cain and Lamech, this *wickedness (rā'ah)* and penchant for *evil (ra')* comes as no surprise. But now things have moved beyond purely individual misdeeds. A language of totality speaks of a new all-time low in corruption shared by all: "*every* inclination...*only* evil *continually.*" This is not the timeless and generalized "original sin" of Christian theology, but a climatic level of communal malevolence that has increased beyond the limits of God's tolerance. Human evil has reached "flood stage." God's reaction is to *blot out* (v. 7), a verb characteristic of the flood story (7:4, 23). This verb is used elsewhere for wiping off a wet dish or wiping away tears or writing.

Step Five: Opposites and Contrasts

Spirit and *flesh* are opposites in the Hebrew Bible. Spirit is divinely strong; flesh is humanly weak. Isaiah 31:3 states this contrast in classic form: "The Egyptians are human, and not God; / their horses are flesh, and not spirit." "My spirit," that is to say God's spirit, is the essence of life that comes from God (Job 33:4; Isa. 42:5) and can be withdrawn by God (Ps. 104:29–30; Eccl. 12:7). At creation, the breath of life came from God (Gen. 2:7).

This is explicitly God's spirit; nothing suggests that it has been introduced into the human gene pool by the sexual activity of the sons of God. This spirit abides in all humankind, not just the offspring of those divine-human intermarriages. Nevertheless, because God's reaction in verse 3 comes immediately after the report of intermarriage in verse 2, clearly some connection between the two events is implied. Mixing the social and sexual spheres of the divine and the human has created some sort of problem, although its precise nature remains unspecified. God responds by restricting the human lifespan, explicitly because humans are flesh (NJB accurately translates "only flesh"). The implication is that flesh is incompatible with divine spirit over the long term. Genesis 3:22 also asserts God's determination that divine and human qualities should be united in humans only for a limited time period.

Flesh is not inherently wicked or negative, but simply characteristic of the weak and ephemeral nature of being human. Even if the products of these mixed marriages share in some sort of godlike nature, they are still basically flesh like all humans; and any entitlement to immortality on their part must be strictly ruled out. The actions of the sons of God have challenged the boundary between the human and divine realms and broken through the frontier separating immortal from mortal and divine from human. In response, God solidifies that boundary for all of humanity by assuring that the interrelationship between divine spirit and human flesh will remain only temporary. Paradoxically (perhaps unfairly, even), the sons of God have committed the boundary violation, but humans must experience lifetimes shorter than the multiple centuries enjoyed by those who lived before the flood (compare Genesis 5).

A powerful rhetorical contrast is drawn between the human heart (v. 5) and God's heart (v. 6). The human heart displays our proclivity for wickedness. God's heart displays God's emotional upset over the need for universal destruction.

Step Six: Characters

The *human women* are merely the objects of the actions of the sons of God and not active characters in their own right. Their contribution to the plot action is limited to being beautiful as objects of male sight and bearing children as a result of male sexual activity ("went in to"). However, it would be an interesting exercise in the interpretive imagination to try to "get into the shoes" of these women who end up as the wives of minor deities and mothers of fabled heroes. What would that have been like? The text itself, given its pro-male, sexist orientation, shows no indication of caring about this question, but we modern readers certainly do. Is it any surprise that only the male offspring of these marriages are mentioned? In Hebrew, these are clearly *male* warrior heroes and *men* of renown.

These *Nephilim,* heroes and famous warriors, are not active characters either. The writer does not seem to want us to pay too much attention to them. That they are the result of the illicit sex initiated by the sons of God seems apparent, but even this is not stated unambiguously. Nor is it necessarily certain that the Nephilim are identical with the heroes and warriors of renown, since one group is mentioned at the start of verse 4 and the other at the end of that verse. Are the Nephilim understood to be part of the problem that God reacts to in verse 3, or simply the natural results of the divine/ human unions that are in themselves the real problem? The only connection drawn between the Nephilim and the reader is that Nephilim are not just figures active "in those days" before the flood, but also have a later history in the conquest period ("and also afterward").

God is the most important and interesting character in this passage. God is the subject of the verbs "said" (vv. 3 and 7), "saw" (v. 5), "be sorry" (vv. 6 and 7), and "blot out" (v. 7). God is committed to preserving the boundary between the divine and the human. Up until now, God has remained engaged with these troublesome humans (3:21; 4:1, 15, 25). But human wickedness and human tendencies have now reached such a low point that God has second thoughts. God moves away from a steadfast commitment to what has been created and adopts a plan for the destruction of all human and animal life. The phrase "I...created" and the language of "animals and creeping things and birds of the air" serves as a cross-reference that takes us back to the creation account of Genesis 1. The author claims to know a great deal about God's inner life, describing God's deepest feelings and giving insight into God's internal thoughts. This marks a huge change in God's attitude, going far beyond God's limited reaction to the misdeeds of Man and Woman or Cain or the sons of God.

Noah is present here, but only briefly. He "found favor" with God (v. 8), but at this point we are not told why. It can hardly be an accident that the consonants of Noah's name spell the Hebrew word for "favor" backwards!

Step Seven: Patterns and Structures

Even though these verses are not tightly organized, unmistakable shapes and patterns still hold them together and give special emphasis to particular elements.

Verses 1–4 are confusing and rather disconnected. Verse 3 seems to have little to do with the episode described in verses 1–2. Why does God take action against humans when the sons of God are the perpetrators? Why is God's decision described before the birth of the Nephilim, who seem to be the focus of the problem? In fact, because verse 3 breaks the connection between illicit sex and the birth of the Nephilim, the verse order 1–2, 4, 3 would actually seem to make more sense. Such an order would also make the 120 year limitation apply more clearly to all humans, Nephilim and ancient heroes included. Nevertheless, verses 1–4 can be understood in their present order as three successive statements on the same subject. They follow a logical, if not chronological, sequence. Verses 1–2 describe an event. Verse 3 reports God's reaction to the event. Verse 4 gives information about the results of the event.

Verses 1–2 hold together nicely as a narrative episode. The sons of God "saw—took—chose" human daughters. To choose implies a certain freedom and unrestrained action on the part of these junior deities and a sharp power differential between them and human beings, particularly human women. This is the only place in the Old Testament where the verb "choose" is used with women as its object. Repeated vocabulary achieves a pleasing sense of unity: "humankind multiplies…daughters are born…daughters of humankind." However, this series of events breaks off abruptly at the end of verse 2. The reader is left hanging. What happened next? What was the result of these sexual relationships?

In verse 3 the spotlight abruptly shifts away from the sons of God and human women to God and God's decision. God speaks, but to no one in particular. "The LORD said" is often used in the Old Testament to describe God's internal self-reflection. The only carryover from verses 1–2 is the word "humankind" (*'ādām*; NRSV "mortals"). Because verse 3 follows verses 1–2, the reader is likely to assume that any offspring of these unions would be potentially immortal or at least live for a enormously long time. But the subject of immortality is never made explicit. Instead, verse 3 introduces the blending of spirit and flesh within the human person as a seemingly new topic. God's announcement is not really a punishment but another move away from extraordinary primeval conditions to humanity's present state of affairs.

Verse 3 is strikingly similar to 3:22 in both form and content. In each verse, God points out a problematic situation and then announces why action is needed. A decisive solution follows:

Then the LORD God said…
the man has become like one of us…
he might…live forever…
the LORD God sent him forth (3:22)

Then the LORD said…
my spirit shall not abide…forever…
for they are flesh…
their days shall be one hundred twenty years (6:3)

God's declaration moves beyond the earlier prevention of immortality (the "forever" of 3:22) to limit human life to a definite maximum (the "not…forever" of 6:3). Again, this is not a punishment so much as a reasonable precaution. Interbreeding between deities and humans has raised the danger that divine spirit would endure in flesh perpetually, but it is the nature of flesh to be bound by time.

Verse 4 does not actually continue the dramatic action of either verses 1–2 or verse 3. Instead, it is an informative background note on the Nephilim, reporting when they flourished and who they were. However, two new pieces of information expand on the marriages reported in verse 2, revealing that the sons of God and human women did have sex and that the women did indeed give birth. However, verse 4 does not come right out and say that the Nephilim were the offspring of the sons of God and human women. It only hints at this by reporting that the Nephilim existed during the time ("in those days") when those acts of mating and birthing were occurring. Then again, the repetition of "the sons of God…the daughters of humans" from verse 2 implies strongly that the Nephilim were indeed the children of their union. Perhaps the writer is trying to downplay their identity as half-divine beings without actually denying their origin.

Verses 5–8 shift gears so that God once again becomes the center of attention. Although this change is abrupt, a few connections hold verses 1–4 and 5–8 together. "The LORD saw" at the start of verse 5 follows verses 2 and 3 as the next episode in a connected chain of events leading up to the flood:

v. 2 the sons of God *saw*
  v. 3 the LORD *said*
v. 5 the LORD *saw*
  v. 7 the LORD *said*

In addition, the phrase "face of the ground" creates an encompassing frame around verses 1–7a (NRSV translates as "the earth" in v. 7). At the beginning, humans multiply *on* it; in the end, they will be blotted out *from* it. Another unifying link is that in verse 1 humanity is multiplying (in Hebrew "becoming *great*"), while in verse 5 the Lord sees that humanity's wickedness is *great.*

Other structuring devices operate within verses 5–8. There is a contrasting balance between the first words and the last: "The LORD saw…wickedness" and "Noah found favor in the sight of the LORD." Verses 6–7 display a pleasing concentric pattern:

A The LORD was sorry that he had made
  B man on the earth
  B' blot out man…from the face of the ground
A' for I am sorry that I have made them. (RSV)

Verses 5–7 move from God's perception of humanity's depravity (described externally in v. 5 and internally in v. 6) to God's announcement of a plan of action to negate it. Verse 8 is attached loosely as a contrast to God's sentence of doom: "*But* Noah." God's reason for blotting out human and animal life is quite explicit, but no reason is given for why Noah is favored, at least at this point. Verse 9 represents a new start with a new introductory formula, "These are the descendants of Noah."

Looking at pronouns in the text, I am struck by "*my* spirit" in verse 3. By speaking in this way, God associates God's very own selfhood with something that animates human life. The first person is also used in verse 7 in God's other speech: "*I* have created...*I* am sorry...*I* have made." This too expresses God's attachment to creation and suggests God's intense emotional involvement in what must be done. "*I* am sorry" personalizes and intensifies the impact of verse 6 ("the Lord was sorry").

Step Eight: Plot Movement

The connection between verses 1–4 and 5–8 is so loose that one has to ask whether the two paragraphs can really work together as a narrative plot. However, if we put together some of the unifying structures noted in the previous section, we discover a remarkable similarity in language. I have provided my own translation of the Hebrew to highlight the parallels:

> *humankind* began to grow *great*
>> on the face of the *ground*
>>> then the Lord God *said*
>>>> my spirit shall not abide in *humankind* (vv. 1, 3)

> the wickedness of *humankind* was *great*
>> in the *earth*
>>> so the Lord *said*
>>>> I will blot out *humankind* (vv. 5, 7)

Because the events of verses 1–4 are reported just before those of verses 5–7, we instinctively interpret the episode of divine-human intermarriage as a source or example of the "wickedness" alleged in verse 5. There are logical problems in doing so, of course. Intermarriage between minor deities and humans is not an especially good illustration of the wicked inclination of human heart, especially since the sons of God are the active perpetrators. Nor does the resulting limit on life span come in response to human wickedness, but is instead a function of the long-term incompatibility of divine spirit and human flesh. In fact, nothing hints at a negative value judgment in verses 1–4, although it is hard to imagine that any Israelite reader would not be made extremely uncomfortable by what these verses report. Only when the reader comes to verses 5–7 and then reflects back on what has already been said does God's response to those divine-human intermarriages begin to sound like a punishment. Only then do the events of verses 1–2 begin to look as if they are illustrations or examples of humanity's inclination to evil. In the absence of clear, well-developed interconnections provided by the text itself, the reader has to do most of the work in constructing a dramatic plot line.

As it unfolds, however, the text does seem to anticipate questions the reader is likely to have. Once upon a time the sons of God could choose women as they pleased, and intermarriages occurred. Could these intermarriages have led to human beings living forever? No, that did not happen, because God declared that the human lifespan would be limited from then on. Do you wonder who the offspring of these unions were? The Nephilim were on the earth in those days. God condemned humanity so totally and extensively that God opted to destroy creation itself. What could have caused such a sweeping judgment? Go back and recall what happened when then sons of God saw the beauty of human women. Then how did humanity come to survive the total catastrophe of the flood? The answer is that "Noah found favor."

Step Nine: Purpose and Intention

At one level, the story answers questions about our present world based on events set in the ancient past. How did the Nephilim and other warrior heroes of our epic songs and stories come into being? Why did even righteous people like Moses live so much shorter lives than the ancients who lived before and just after the flood? Why did the flood take place, and how did humanity survive it?

The flood myths of Mesopotamia usually have the problem of human overpopulation as one of their themes. The gods typically send the flood to limit the numbers of burgeoning humanity and the noise they make. Genesis 6 also provides subtle hints of the topic of overpopulation. "When people began to multiply" at least suggests this. Setting a limit to the human lifespan could be understood as a way of limiting human population growth. Perhaps by resolving any suggestion of the danger of overpopulation in this less drastic way, the author was trying to prevent readers familiar with Mesopotamian parallels from downgrading the flood into nothing more than God's way of controlling overpopulation. On the contrary, God sent the flood in response to extreme wickedness and pervasive evil inclinations.

Step Ten: Text in Context

This striking episode provides us with instructions on how to read what has gone before and what will happen next. It encourages us to interpret the previous stories of Genesis 2–4 as an unbroken string of human failures, to evaluate the flood as a completely justified reaction to human depravity, and to understand humanity's survival as the result of God's surprising benevolence to Noah.

Genesis 6:1–8 shifts the focus of the ongoing story from a few individuals living in families (Genesis 2–4) to people proliferating into a larger population. This focus on bigger groups will continue in 9:18–27 (ethnic groups determined by genealogical descent) and 11:1–9 (national groups determined by language).

Familiar themes appear. The boundary separating the divine and the human had been endangered when the first humans sought to be like God and Woman *saw* the tree as *good* and *took* from it (3:5–6). In Genesis 6 this boundary is threatened by an encroachment from the other direction, as minor deities *take* human women whom they *see* to be *good* (6:2; NRSV "fair"). Multiplication "on the face of the ground" looks back to the expansion of the human population described in Genesis 4 and 5 and looks forward to the dispersal of the people of Babel "over the face of all the earth" (11:9). "Warriors of renown" are literally "men of name." We are reminded that Cain sought to perpetuate the name of his son through a city (4:17) and that gaining a famous name will also motivate the citizens of Babel to build their city (11:4). God imposes successive limitations on human existence. First, we were barred from Eden and the tree of life. Now we live for only a brief period. In Genesis 11, our cooperative efforts and ability to stay concentrated together will be stymied by dispersal and language confusion.

Genesis 6:5–7 and 8:21 create a "before and after" framework around the flood. Both at the beginning and the end of the flood, God makes a "heartfelt" mid-course correction in the divine plan for creation. Before the flood we read:

> The LORD saw...that every *inclination* of the thoughts of their *hearts* was only *evil* continually. And the LORD was sorry...and

it grieved him to his *heart.* So the LORD said, "I will blot out…"
(6:5–7)

When the flood has passed, God's plans have changed:

> The LORD said in his *heart,* "I will never again curse the ground
> because of humankind, for the *inclination* of the human *heart*
> is *evil* from youth; nor will I ever again destroy…" (8:21)

Remarkably, God's decision to send a flood and the decision never
again to do so are both based on the evil inclination of the human
heart. Humanity has not changed its ways; what has changed is the
response of God's heart.

Step Eleven: Claims and Assertions

First, this text claims that certain set parameters limit the institution
of marriage. These grotesque divine/human marriage alliances
contradict the structure of marriage that God set up in 2:21–24.
Admittedly, these unions are like proper marriages with sexual
attraction, sexual union, and the resultant birthing of children.
However, these partners are not of the same "bone and flesh," and
their joining can hardly be said to result in "one flesh." Moreover,
unlike what is proclaimed in 2:24 and 3:16, nothing is said here
about mutual attraction. The sons of God do all the seeing, taking,
choosing, and "going in to."

Second, this episode explores something of what it means to be a
sinful human before God. Some interpreters read these stories in terms
of a snowballing increase of human sin in the world and thus
understand the episode of the sons of God as the worst example yet
of an escalating growth in sin. I disagree. It is hard to maintain that
human transgression grows worse and worse as we move from Eve to
Cain to Lamech to this particular episode. Indeed humans in 6:1–4
are the victims of disorder, not its perpetrators. Instead, it is better to
see this incident as providing yet another example of the variety of
ways that sin can appear. Nevertheless, it is the example that
immediately precedes the flood. Intermarriage with the sons of God
may or may not be a worse example of evil than murder by Cain or
Lamech's violent song, but it does seem to serve as the culminating
event that tips the balance with God. From God's perspective, it is the
last straw.

Third, this story claims that God has placed limitations on human
potentials. God will not allow powerful, superhuman spirit to empower

our weak human flesh for too long. Unlike the sons of God, we do not live forever. Our achievements and heroics are necessarily limited by our fleeting lifespan, even if we are "warriors of renown."

Fourth, God's grace and patience can be exhausted. Verses 5–8 offer the most negative evaluation of the human condition to be found in the entire Old Testament. Humans have wicked hearts. They are close to being totally corrupt: "every inclination…only evil continually." All the negative characteristics of humanity, hinted at in the previous stories of disobedience and violence, now have come to a head. Now God is sorry and intends to blot out creation. God's reaction is more radical and negative at this point than anything the reader of Genesis has encountered or will encounter. The curses announced in Genesis 3 and 4 or the confusion and scattering imposed upon the citizens of Babel pale into nothingness behind God's ultimate threat, "I will blot out."

Fifth, God is emotionally involved in the human story and does not choose to "let go." Verses 5–7 report a decisive inner change for the worse in God's attitude towards humanity. The wicked heart of humanity has caused a grieved heart in God. Yet even in the ultimate crisis of a decision to "blot out," verse 8 asserts that God remained committed to humanity. Noah found favor. God has second thoughts and regrets having created humans, but still remains the God who provided Adam and Eve with clothes, protected Cain with a mark, and provided Seth as a new seed to counter the line of Cain and Lamech. The favor Noah finds in God's eyes hints at the promise of a new start in spite of humanity's heart inclined to evil.

Sixth and quite paradoxically, this text uses a polytheistic myth to promote the uniqueness and sole power of the One God. These secondary, junior-grade deities are merely "bit players" in a drama in which God is the sole decisive actor. God pays no attention to their improper antics and does not refer to them in any way. God is the only speaker and decisively causes important events through announcements in the first person singular: "my spirit," "I am sorry that I have made," and "I will blot out."

Sources

References to the pre-flood giants appear in the Apocrypha: Wisdom of Solomon 14:6; Sirach 16:7; Baruch 3:26; 3 Maccabees 2:4. Early Jewish texts about "fallen angels" who left heaven to mate with human women include Jubilees 5:1–11; 1 Enoch 6–19, 86–88; 2 Enoch 18; Testament of Reuben 5:6.

My understanding of verses 1–4 was informed by Franz H. Breukelman, "The Story of the Sons of God Who Took the Daughters of Humans as Wives," in *Voices from Amsterdam*, ed. Martin Kessler (Atlanta: Scholars Press, 1994), 83–94, and Marc Vervenne, "All They Need Is Love: Once More Genesis 6:1–4," in *Words Remembered, Texts Renewed: Essays in Honour of John F. A. Sawyer*, ed. Jon Davies *et al.* (Sheffield: Sheffield Academic Press, 1995), 19–40.

CHAPTER 7

Drunk with New Wine

Genesis 9:18–27

Step One: Bracket Off What You "Know"

Now that the flood is over, one might think that the problem of human misconduct has been solved, or at least moderated. What a shock it is to read this narrative about drunkenness, dishonor, and slavery!

You may not know this story well and probably do not like what you do know. Over the centuries, interpreters have repeatedly manipulated this story for their own ends. Some Americans before the Civil War used it to justify slavery, and it played a similar role in South Africa as a rationalization for apartheid. These interpreters assumed that Ham was the ancestor of black Africans. Because of his wicked deed, a curse of slavery supposedly affected all his descendants. Such a reading was comfortable for slave owners since it suggested that Africans were naturally intended to be slaves. That Noah actually cursed Ham's son *Canaan* rather than Ham himself was not necessarily seen as undermining this interpretation. This text could still be used, along with Joshua's curse on the Gibeonites (Josh. 9:23, 27), to justify slavery in general as a divinely approved social institution, without any need to draw a genealogical connection between Canaan or Ham and black Africans.

113

Given our own contemporary obsessions, modern interpreters often read this story in ways that expose supposedly concealed issues of sexuality. The language of "uncovering nakedness" is used in Leviticus to describe incestuous sexual relations (Lev. 18:6–17, especially v. 7; 20:17). On this basis, interpreters have imagined a homosexual encounter between Ham and Noah, sexual contact between Ham and some unmentioned second wife of Noah, or even Ham's castration of his father. None of this makes much sense based on the story that is actually on the page in front of us. There is nothing metaphorical or symbolic about the nakedness of Genesis 9:22. Shem and Japheth physically cover their father's completely literal nakedness, walking backward so they could not see it.

Step Two: What Is Familiar?

We know about the problematic effects of too much alcohol and that drinking too much leads to shameful situations (Lam. 4:21; Hab. 2:15). We are also familiar with intergenerational conflicts, irresponsible youngest sons, and the power of a father's curse to set the course of a family's future. Family systems theory teaches us that the effects of family dysfunction can reverberate negatively down through generations. Inappropriate nakedness still has power to disrupt social stability. Even the ready accessibility of nudity in movies, magazines, and on the Internet has not robbed it of its force.

Nor is slavery unknown to us. If we are Americans, the insidious poison of past slavery still affects our national life. Contemporary slavery still exists in parts of Africa, and the news media report occasional examples even in Europe and North America.

Did you look up Shem, Ham, and Japheth in a Bible dictionary? Genesis 10, known as the Table of Nations, describes their supposed descendants in terms of the ancient nations known to Israel. Japheth represents Mediterranean Europe and Asia Minor; Ham corresponds to Egypt, North Africa and southern Arabia; and Shem personifies Mesopotamia. This tripartite division was based on political affiliation and approximate geography rather than actual biological descent. The peoples assigned to Ham seem to have been under Egypt's political or cultural influence. Ham and Shem overlap in the Arabian Peninsula. Social organization also seems to have played a role in the construction of this table. Shem represents tribally organized nomads and semi-nomads while Ham stands for the urban sedentary populations of Egypt and Mesopotamia (compare the Hamite Nimrod's kingdom in 10:10–12).

We are familiar with the idea of a world divided by geography, ethnicity, and culture. We speak of the West over against non-Western cultures and of the economic disparity between South and North. Enslavement of one set of nations to another may remind modern readers of the colonialism of the nineteenth and twentieth centuries as well as post-colonialist structures that still maintain previous patterns of economic dependency and exploitation. Viewed from this perspective, Shem and Japheth could be seen as corresponding in some ways to today's "first world," while Ham corresponds to the developing "two-thirds world."

We tend to divide the world's peoples by race, a classification that has its roots in both genetic and social factors. Whether we like it or not, race has almost always been connected with status. There are parallels between present-day notions of race and the story of Noah's sons, although it should be emphasized that the classification of races we use cannot be coordinated with Shem, Ham, and Japheth in any way. At the same time, both Genesis and we agree that all humans are so closely related that we can be regarded as a single family.

Noah's wish is that God will expand Japheth's territory. We are well acquainted with the widespread desire of nations and peoples to expand into unsettled areas or to appropriate the lands of neighboring peoples.

Step Three: What Is Unfamiliar?

Our ideas of humanity's genetic and cultural interrelationships are much more complicated than the simple family tree of Noah's three sons.

The careful reader will notice a gap in the story. How did Noah find out what Ham had done to him while he was unconscious? Such silences are quite common in biblical stories and apparently indicate that the author did not consider the missing information important.

Our two biggest puzzles are likely to be: What exactly did Ham do wrong? and, Why does Noah curse Canaan when it was Ham who committed the misdeed?

Let us look first at Ham's offense. Israelite culture took personal honor and shame very seriously. Israelites were also much less tolerant of bodily exposure than we are. Ham shamed Noah, not only by allowing himself to look at his father in a drunken, uncovered state, but also by telling his brothers about it. In contrast, Shem and Japheth illustrate what Ham should have done. They carefully avoided looking at their father, but covered him up instead. Thus Ham failed to take appropriate action when he came upon a situation that brought shame on his father. Dishonoring one's parent is the exact opposite of a basic principle of Israelite morality, "Honor your father and your mother" (Ex. 20:12). The deadly seriousness of shaming one's parents is shown by the law recorded in Deuteronomy 21:18–21.

There seems to be a sharp break between Genesis 9:24 and 25. When Noah finds out what his "youngest son" Ham has done, he condemns Canaan to be a slave to "his brothers." One source of confusion for the reader is that Noah's other two sons are described as Canaan's brothers. Was Ham actually the one cursed in some lost, earlier version of this story? In any case, the present shape of the story raises a more pressing problem. Why does Noah lay this curse on Canaan rather than Ham? Some rabbis and early church fathers suggested that Noah could not curse Ham because God had already blessed him in 9:1. Augustine instead saw this as an example of the effect of original sin on subsequent generations. It is more likely, however, that the explanation should be sought in Israel's family-oriented view of punishment and in its deep-seated hostility to the Canaanites.

In Israel, the reckoning for a misdeed could sometimes turn out to be a family matter. The Ten Commandments suggest that the sins of parents might have a negative impact on their children's lives (Ex. 20:5). The death of the first child born to the illicit union of David and Bathsheba provides a good example of this sort of thinking (2 Sam. 12:15–23). Ham as son has dishonored his father Noah. This offense is appropriately punished by a curse on Ham's son, which brings dishonor on Ham. Just as Noah has been shamed as father by the actions of his son Ham, so Ham as father will be shamed by the humiliation of his son Canaan.

Even though Israelites and Canaanites were actually closely related to each other in culture and language, Old Testament texts reveal the contempt in which Canaanites were held. The Canaanites were heirs to a long-standing system of urban culture that had been destabilized when Israel emerged as a competing rural village culture in the highlands of Palestine. According to texts such as Deuteronomy 12:29–31, Canaanite religious practices involved sexuality and infant sacrifice that would lead Israel astray. Therefore the Canaanites and their religion were to be utterly destroyed (Deut. 7:2–5, 25–26; 12:2–3; 20:16–18). Although the Canaanites were never actually wiped out, Israel made at least some Canaanites into slaves (Josh. 16:10; 17:13;

Judg. 1:28, 30, 33, 35). Solomon did the same thing, drafting them to work on royal building projects (1 Kings 9:20–21). The story of the curse on Canaan must be connected with Israel's historical disdain for and subjugation of the Canaanites.

Step Four: Key Words

Your list of repeated words should include *son, father, brother, tent, nakedness,* and *slave.*

This is a family story about *fathers, sons,* and *brothers.* Noah is, of course, the father whose honor is damaged by one son and shielded by his other sons. However, rather surprisingly, the fatherhood of Ham is actually mentioned first and emphasized by repetition. Each time Ham is mentioned by name he is identified as "the father of Canaan" (vv. 18 and 22). Being Canaan's father is clearly fundamental to Ham's identity as far as this story is concerned. The phrase "father of Canaan" also implies that Ham epitomizes what his descendant Canaan will be and do as a historical people (compare Jabal and Jubal in 4:20–21). These two references to Canaan in verses 18 and 22 help prepare the reader for the curveball that the story throws when Noah curses Canaan instead of Ham. The text also emphasizes from the start that the three brothers are the *sons* of Noah (vv. 18 and 19), perhaps asking the reader to consider how well they will discharge their respective filial responsibilities. The designation *youngest son* in verse 24 emphasizes Ham's shortfall in this particular regard.

Wine surrounds the episode of Noah's shame. Drinking wine leads to his lying uncovered (v. 21; another translation is "uncovered himself" NJPS). Awaking from his wine leads to him knowing what his son had done (v. 24). Israelite readers might have expected that any story that starts in a vineyard would turn out be a positive one. Vineyards, vines, and wine were associated with rest, joy, and sensual delight (Judg. 9:13; Ps. 104:15; Song 7:12; Isa. 25:6). Vine and vineyard symbolized Israel as God's people (Isa. 5:1–7; 27:2–6; Jer. 2:21; 12:10). Instead of the positive aspects of the vineyard, however, Noah the novice drinker experiences the proverbial downside of wine (Prov. 20:1; 21:17; 23:30–31). Similar to cities and the other new discoveries and technologies described in Genesis 4:20–22 and 11:3, Israel did not consider the secret of making wine as a gift from the gods, as did some surrounding cultures, but a purely human accomplishment.

Tent occurs both as the location of Noah's humiliation (9:21) and as Japheth's fortunate residence in the territory of Shem (v. 27). In the first instance, the word indicates that Noah was not lying exposed for all to see, but that Ham had to violate Noah's privacy and seclusion to peep at his father. In verse 27 *tent* indicates the pastoral, semi-nomadic lifestyle of the descendants of Shem. To live in the tents of a group was to share their territory and ways (1 Chr. 5:10; Ps. 84:10).

Nakedness is associated with shame (Isa. 47:2; Lam. 1:8; 4:21). The word is used once to indicate Ham's impropriety (v. 22), but twice to emphasize his brothers' contrasting proper behavior. They both "covered" nakedness and "did not see" it (v. 23). This is a different word than that used for the nakedness of Man and Woman in Genesis 2–3, focusing more specifically on the genitals and sexuality.

The word *slave* in the Old Testament describes individuals who were legally owned by another to whom they owed full-time labor, either permanently or (in the case of a fellow Israelite) for a term of years. It also refers to groups of people conscripted to work on government projects. The Hebrews were slaves in Egypt in this latter sense. The expression translated "lowest of slaves" (v. 25) is literally "slave of slaves" (compare "king of kings" or "song of songs" to mean the greatest king and the greatest song). Repetition of the same words at the conclusion of verses 26 and 27 strongly emphasizes Canaan's slave status.

Step Five: Opposites and Contrasts

Three pairs of contrasting notions relate to Noah's dishonor, Ham's misdeed, and the other two sons' honorable response:

- *Drunk* (v. 21) is opposed to *awoke* and *knew* (v. 24).
- *Uncovered* (v. 21) is opposed to *covered* (v. 23).
- *Saw the nakedness of his father* (v. 22) is opposed to *did not see their father's nakedness* (v. 23).

In regard to the last of these, sometimes merely looking at something inappropriate could transgress a boundary that ought to remain inviolate. Thus Lot's wife looked back at Sodom (Gen. 19:26). Seeing God could be mortally dangerous (Ex. 33:20; Judg. 6:22; 13:22). Boundaries could be violated in the opposite direction as well. Allowing one's nakedness (genitals) *to be seen* in the context of sacrificial worship was a serious breach of propriety (Ex. 20:26).

Another set of opposites involves *blessing* and *curse* and the future fate of Shem and Japheth in contrast to that of Canaan. In the world of the Old Testament, curses and blessings were not merely empty wishes or expectant prayers. When spoken by someone who had the proper authority, curses and blessings were words of effective power, inevitably and automatically accomplishing positive or negative effects upon those targeted. Fathers had the authority and the responsibility to bless their sons. Isaac blessed Jacob and Esau with blessings of different worth (Gen. 27:27–29, 39–40). Jacob does the same with his sons and grandsons (48:14–20; Genesis 49). These blessings establish the future destiny of the descendants of those blessed, some less positively than others. As is often true in our world, the blessing of one group sometimes seems to entail the curse of another (25:23; 27:29, 40; 49:15).

The curse and blessing that shape the future relationships of Shem, Japheth, and Canaan are effective and powerful because Noah speaks them in his role as patriarch and father. Unlike the curses God proclaimed in 3:14 and 4:11–12, Canaan's fate is not presented as *divine* punishment but as the result of a *human* pronouncement. Noah's curse may be compared to Adam's words about Eve (3:20) and Eve's words about Seth (4:25). Interpreters often overlook this and speak without justification about God's curse on Canaan. Nevertheless, the reader is still likely to understand these words as powerful and effective pronouncements because Noah speaks them as ancestor of all the world's peoples and because they were uttered in the formative period of primeval beginnings.

The two blessings are different in wording and nature. The first uses the verb "bless." The second is still a blessing but uses the less direct language of wish (compare Gen. 24:60; 27:28; 28:3–4). The first blessing ties Shem's future well-being directly to the Lord. The second subordinates Japheth's welfare to that of Shem ("in the tents"). Even though the two brothers both performed the same upright deed and both are to gain advantage from Canaan's servitude, Noah gives Shem precedence. If we put the information of 9:24 and 10:21 together, Shem would be the eldest son. However, the specific reason for Shem's priority in this particular story is his special relationship to God. Because Shem was viewed as the ancestor of Israel, Israelite readers would have received a strong confirmation of their identity as God's people.

A problem in verse 26 requires special comment. Because Hebrew was originally written in a way that did not specify every vowel sound, sometimes we have more than one way to understand a passage. The NRSV translates Noah's words about Shem as an expectation of direct divine blessing, "Blessed by the LORD my God be Shem." This is certainly a possible translation and provides a somewhat better parallel to the blessing of Japheth. However, the traditional and more natural way to read verse 26 is, "Blessed be the LORD, God of Shem" (NJB, NJPS; NAB; NIV). The phrase "blessed be the LORD" is used elsewhere to praise God for some gracious action that has already been performed (Gen. 24:27; Ex. 18:10; Ruth 4:14). According to this second translation possibility, Noah blesses God in anticipation of a gracious relationship that still remains undefined and unstated. Nevertheless, the difference in meaning between these two translations is not great. To bless someone's God is to bless that person.

Step Six: Characters

Although the story begins with Noah's drunkenness, the reader soon discovers that it is really about Ham's misdeed in contrast to the honorable behavior of Shem and Japheth and about the future effects of their differing conduct on their descendants.

Noah is associated with the ground (v. 20; NRSV "soil") and so parallels Adam (3:17) and Cain (4:3) as an agriculturalist. In connection with 5:29 and 8:21, this may be seen as a positive development in that God's curse on the ground (3:17; 4:11) now seems to have been moderated somewhat. Noah is presented sympathetically. We readers expect that his sons will honor him and not shame him, even if he should happen to experience a bad episode involving his pioneering experiment in winemaking. Although the text does not explicitly say that this was his first experience with alcohol, the close connection between verses 20 and 21 make it easy for the reader to assume this. As the ancestor of all three divisions of humanity, Noah has the authority to curse and bless their respective destinies.

Ham's name may mean "uncle" or "paternal relative." By making him the youngest son (v. 24), the story suggests that we should not be so surprised that he proves to be Noah's problem child.

Japheth's future is already reflected in his name, understood in this text to mean, "may he enlarge." By this is meant "make space for him" or "extend his boundaries." An increase in territory would be seen as a positive development for a multiplying agricultural people (Gen. 26:22; Deut. 12:20). Japheth is to be the co-enslaver of Canaan with Shem and will be intermingled with and neighbor to Shem ("in the tents of Shem"). It is unclear what period of history is intended by this description. Scholars often suggest the time of Solomon, whose realm included numerous foreign peoples and who put the Canaanites to forced labor on government projects (1 Kings 9:20–21).

The Lord is the God of Shem in a special way (translating v. 26 as "God of Shem"). Israelite readers would automatically identify themselves with Shem as their ancestor (Gen. 11:10–32). The English "Semite" and "Semitic" derive from the equivalent of Shem in the Latin Bible.

The threefold expression "Shem, Ham, and Japheth" encompasses all of humanity from a worldwide standpoint. But from the narrower perspective of Israel living in Palestine, it is specifically *Canaan* and Canaan's status that would be most important for the original readers. Ancient peoples like the Israelites tended to conceive of political and ethnic relationships in terms of descent and genealogy. Because the territory of Canaan and the Canaanite cities had been under the domination of Egypt before Israel appeared on the scene, it was natural to classify both Egypt and Canaan as sons of Ham (10:6). The Philistines were linked politically with Egypt and so were cataloged as descendants of Ham as well (10:14).

Canaan as an individual stands for Canaan as a people, just as Ishmael stands for the Ishmaelites, Jacob (whose other name was Israel) stands for Israel, and Esau (also called Edom) stands for the Edomites. National groups were understood to be the literal descendants of founding individuals, whom scholars label "eponymous ancestors." Thus the Romans traced their ancestry back to Romulus and the Greeks (that is, the Hellenes) to one Hellen, son of the only couple to survive a great flood sent by Zeus.

God, too, is a character in this story, but remains completely offstage throughout. God is invoked in the blessings spoken by Noah, but significantly *not* in his curse on Canaan. Because Noah has the authority to bless, the reader naturally assumes that God will bring good things to Shem and territorial enlargement to Japheth. But it is important that Noah does not connect God directly to the future enslavement of Canaan's descendants.

Step Seven: Patterns and Structures

Verses 18–19 build a bridge back to the flood story. Noah's three sons (5:32; 6:10) had gone into the ark (8:16, 18), and now they come out of it. The introductory verse 18 is connected to the story that follows by the phrase "father of Canaan" applied to Ham, which appears a second time in verse 22.

The main action of the story is enclosed by the phrases "drank some of the wine" (v. 21) and "awoke from his wine" (v. 24). "Some of" and "from" are the same preposition in Hebrew.

The contrast between Ham and his two brothers is sharp. Their appropriate actions shed light on, interpret, and judge Ham's inappropriate behavior. In literary terms, Shem and Japheth serve as a "foil" to Ham, highlighting his character and actions by presenting the opposite. This contrast is set forth by means of a reversed pattern and a threefold repetition of "nakedness of his/their father" (translation presented in the original Hebrew word order):

"*saw* the nakedness of his father…and told" (v. 22)
"covered the nakedness of their father…and the nakedness of
    their father they did *not see*" (v. 23)

Ham dishonors his father by seeing and telling; his brothers preserve Noah's honor because they cover him and do not see.

Comparison between the curse and the blessings is encouraged by introducing them with the same words, "he said" (vv. 25 and 26, NRSV adds "also"). At the same time, comparison between the two blessings is encouraged by the repeated refrain "let Canaan be his slave," which strongly emphasizes that this is a most important future development. The repetition of "God" helps solidify the connection between the blessings, while setting them off from the curse, which does not mention God. There is wordplay between "God of Shem" (v. 26, NRSV "my God be Shem") and "tents of Shem" (v. 27). The words "tents" and "God" are similar in Hebrew except for two reversed consonants.

Step Eight: Plot Movement

The story divides into two parts: action (vv. 18–24) and speech (vv. 25–27). Verse 24 is the hinge on which the two parts turn. At this point, Noah returns from his unconsciousness to take part in the story and shifts from action to speech ("he awoke…he knew…he said"). It could be argued that the active part of the story exists only to set up the situation for Noah's speech, which would be the main focus of interest for later readers who were the beneficiaries of Noah's curse and blessing.

Verses 18–20 are exposition. They introduce the characters (Noah and three sons from the ark whose offspring will repopulate the earth) and set the scene (Noah's vineyard). "Father of Canaan" in verse 18 alerts the reader to pay special attention to Ham in what will follow. Verse 19 tells us that this story is going to have an effect on our world. What happens to this family will happen to us, demographically and sociologically.

The story's problem emerges in verses 21–22. There are really two problems, nakedness and shame. "Vineyard" leads to "wine," which leads to "became drunk," which leads to "uncovered" (nakedness) and on to "saw the nakedness" (shame). Ham's act of telling his brothers increases the shame that he heaps on Noah, but also provides a transition to the next episode (vv. 23–27) in which the complementary problems of nakedness and shame are each resolved in turn.

The two virtuous brothers resolve the first problem, that of Noah's uncovered nakedness, by covering it. The text carefully emphasizes their propriety while doing so ("walked backward...faces turned away...did not see") in contrast to Ham's improper actions ("Ham...saw"). However, Noah comes to know what has happened, and so the second problem, that of his shame, remains. Noah counteracts the shame he has suffered by a retaliatory curse on the offender's son and two blessings. Both curse and blessings shame Ham by bringing about the enslavement of his son Canaan. The curse does so directly. The blessings achieve this same goal in a roundabout way, by making Canaan's enslavement an element of the privileged circumstances forecast for Shem and Japheth. The threefold repetition of Noah's nakedness (vv. 22–23) is thus balanced by a threefold reference to Canaan's slavery (vv. 25–27).

Tales told in popular culture often share standard plot elements. The story of Lot and his daughters in Genesis 19:31–38 exhibits several parallels with the story of Noah and his sons. Lot and his daughters are the sole survivors from a catastrophe sent by God's judgment (Sodom). Lot becomes drunk (by his daughters' design), and then they violate proper sexual boundaries to get pregnant by him. Future ethnic groups, in this case the Moabite and Ammonite nations, are the result.

Step Nine: Purpose and Intention

By now you are familiar with the etiological or explanatory function of these early stories from Genesis. The tale of Noah's drunkenness declares that the unequal social relationships and hostilities among ethnic groups known to the first readers are the result of past events. This episode answers important questions for early readers. First, who first invented viniculture and discovered the intoxicating properties of wine? Second, when and how did the social institution of slavery begin? Third, why have the Canaanites become subservient to us and sometimes perform forced labor for us? Fourth, why do we share the land of Canaan and our domination of the Canaanites with certain other peoples we think of as descended from Japheth? It is also likely that this story was remembered and retold to explain why Canaanite slaves were not automatically given their freedom after seven years of service the way Hebrew slaves were (Ex. 21:2–6; Deut. 15:12–18).

Another effect of this story would be to instill the importance of "honoring father and mother" among both children and adults. A review of Old Testament laws reveals that problems in this area arose chiefly in conflicts between adult children and parents who still held some authority over them (for example, Ex. 21:15, 17; Deut. 21:18–21). Shem and Japheth honored their father and were rewarded by his potent blessing. Ham violated this duty and suffered shame in the form of his son's humiliation. Remember that even aged and feeble parents have the power to bless or curse and act accordingly!

This story would strengthen the ethnic identity and pride of Israelite readers and give them a positive sense of destiny as God's people. They were preordained to dominate the Canaanites and be senior partners to whatever peoples descended from Japheth lived in their midst.

Step Ten: Text in Context

There are parallels between this story and some of the others we are looking at. The theme of "first beginnings" continues (4:26; 6:1; 9:20; 11:6). The Noah story represents a breakdown in family solidarity similar to what happens between Cain and Abel. Both stories end in a curse that affects the characters' descendants.

The story of Noah's sons also corresponds to the Eden narrative. Each begins with the planting of a garden or vineyard, but consuming their fruit leads to trouble. Vineyards and gardens were similar locations: protected by walls (Num. 22:24; Song 4:12; Isa. 5:5), well-watered (Gen. 13:10; Isa. 27:2–3; Ezek. 19:10), and places of sensual joy (Song 4:16; 6:2; 7:12). Both Adam and Noah are initiators in cultivating the ground (Gen. 3:23; 9:20). "Nakedness," "seeing," and "knowing" are key elements in each plot. The fact of nakedness can be "told" (3:11; 9:22) and ought to be covered by clothing (3:7, 21; 9:23). In each story, human trespass results in a curse, spoken in Eden by God and then after the flood by Noah. These parallels communicate that humanity's new start after the flood should not be taken to mean that humans have changed their basic nature or inclinations. Eden's negative consequences have not been transcended.

Step Eleven: Claims and Assertions

Some things reflected in this story are simply just true whether we like it or not. The peoples of the earth are marked off into different categories. Some ethnic groups have dominated others and still do so today. Slavery and colonialism have been features of this domination, and the toxic aftereffects of these institutions still pollute contemporary relationships between peoples.

This story can be dreadfully dangerous if read in a proud and ethnocentric way. On the surface, at least, it seems to justify the notion that some ethnic groups are destined to be superior to others. It certainly intends to validate the slavery of the Canaanites to the Israelites, or at least demands that Canaanites submit to temporary forced labor. But does it authorize the enslavement or domination of one people by another in some more general or universal sense?

This narrative becomes dangerous when we take it as a prescription for what should be rather than as a description of what has taken place. It describes the domination and slavery of one ethnic group, the Canaanites, at one period in the past. There is no warrant in the story to generalize that single historical calamity into a universal principle. The Canaanites all disappeared from history a long time ago. Moreover, the narrative does not suggest that slavery or domination is somehow God's will or God's plan. Curse and blessing come from the mouth of Noah, the recently drunk and grievously dishonored parent, not from the mouth of God.

A second great danger occurs when we read this story from a self-interested and ethnocentric viewpoint. A good rule of thumb is, if your interpretation of the Bible makes you feel good about yourselves and superior to others, watch out! If we identify ourselves with Shem or Japheth, we will be tempted to read this story as consolation and reassurance. We may conclude that the Bible proclaims that the world's economic and political structures, through which we dominate other nations and races and from which we so richly benefit, are something predictable. If predictable, we think, then they must be inevitable, acceptable, and even justifiable. Therefore, we may relax and enjoy the status quo.

A healthy antidote to this would be to read as though we were members of an oppressed or marginalized people or of a formerly enslaved race. Obviously, this will really be the case for those of us who are women or homosexuals or belong to a racial or ethnic minority. Reading from this perspective, we find ourselves identifying more easily with Ham and Canaan. This may still prove difficult, however, given what Ham does and who Canaan is. Nevertheless, "reading as Canaanites" can teach us to look beneath the surface of this story, to look at it from the underside. In so doing we may discover that we object to the basic unfairness of punishing Canaan for Ham's crime, to say nothing of the injustice of subjugating whole peoples to oppression for countless generations to produce blessing for others.

Reading from the underside, of course, has its own dangers. We may come to feel that we are morally superior to the Shems and Japheths of this world. Certainly, those who oppress others and those who benefit from the structures of oppression are morally wrong and deserve to be blamed. However, this particular narrative is not so simple when it comes to the question of culpability. We need to remember that Ham is the actual wrongdoer here. Canaan suffers as a result of what Ham did, not because of the actions of his virtuous and dutiful brothers.

The real victim here is Canaan, who pays the price for actions taken by his father and decisions made by his grandfather. Canaan is entangled in a situation created by previous generations and past historical events. When it comes to issues of economic disparity and low social status, people have a tendency to "blame the victim." However, it is impossible to blame Canaan for his fate. He is a pawn of forces and decisions completely beyond his control. If anything, this text offers support for oppressed peoples and suggests that we should blame those who have the opportunity to take action and the power to make decisions that can undo the unjust status quo.

In any case, if we learn nothing else, we at least can take to heart this story's basic presupposition. All peoples and races are literally brothers and sisters, offspring of the same parental line. All of us have been rescued from the same terrible catastrophe. All of us are caught up into the same oppressive social and economic systems.

Sources

On the "curse of Ham," see Gene Rice, "The Curse That Never Was (Genesis 9:18–27)," *Journal of Religious Thought* 29 (1972): 5–27, and Stephen R. Haynes, *Noah's Curse: The Biblical Justification of American Slavery* (New York: Oxford University Press, 2002). I used Marc Vervenne, "What Shall We Do with the Drunken Sailor? A Critical Re-examination of Genesis 9.20–27," *JSOT* 68 (1995): 33–55; Gunther Wittenberg, "'Let Canaan Be His Slave' (Gen. 9.26): Is Ham Also Cursed?" *Journal of Theology for Southern Africa* 74 (1991): 46–56; and A. Tomasino, "History Repeats Itself: The 'Fall' and 'Noah's Drunkenness,'" *VT* 42 (1992): 128–30.

CHAPTER 8

From Babel to Babble

Genesis 11:1–9

Step One: Bracket Off What You "Know"

The way I remember this story from Sunday school is that the inhabitants of this city were possessed by "towering arrogance." They sought to assault God's heavenly realm by raising a tower that reached into heaven, something like the lofty vine in the *Jack and the Beanstalk* story, or Jacob's ladder. To stop their incursion into heaven and punish their pride, God went down to destroy their tower.

However, a careful and slow reading shows that my childhood impressions were not entirely accurate. The text does not mention sin or pride, nor is God's action characterized as punishment. The building project does not seem to be directed against God or initiated as an assault on heaven, but is something the city dwellers do to prevent dispersal and loss of unity. God takes no action to destroy the tower or the city. Instead the conclusion simply states that the city remained unfinished. Here the text says nothing whatsoever about the tower. In fact, the tower itself doesn't seem to be especially important. It is presented merely as an accompanying feature of the city and disappears from view after verse 5. The primary emphasis is on God's confusion of human language and the scattering of humanity out from a single city to the ends of the earth. This confusion and scattering is presented less as a punishment than as a preemptive restriction intended to limit human tendencies and plans that would block God's will for them and the earth.

Most Christians have interpreted this tale as a story of human arrogance and divine punishment, and the traditional title "Tower of Babel" reflects this. However, Jewish interpreters have tended to emphasize the dispersion of humanity and the city dwellers' attempt to prevent it. Jewish tradition calls this story the "Generation of Division." One might say that Christian interpretation has focused on the vertical dimensions of the story, while Jewish interpretation has concentrated on its horizontal aspects. Christians have tended to see humanity's dispersal as a punishment. Jews have understood it to be a divinely premeditated necessity.

Step Two: What Is Familiar?

First, we are familiar with migration. This story begins when humans "struck camp" (NRSV "migrated"), discovered a new plain, and settled there (v. 2). It is unclear whether their movement is "in the east" (REB; NAB), "eastwards" (NJB; NIV), or "from the east" (NRSV; NJPS). In the context of Genesis, this migration is part of a larger story of human expansion and movement that begins when God evicts Man and Woman from Eden and drives Cain away (3:24; 4:16). It continues with population increase before the flood (6:1) and the departure of the sons of Noah from the ark to populate the earth (9:18–19). Migration, immigration, and resettlement have gone on throughout history and continue today.

Second, we know that the settlement of new frontiers often requires new technologies. In the Arctic north, this meant warm clothing made from fur, new ways of constructing shelter, and hunting techniques that could produce a diet high in calories. In nineteenth-century North America, this meant steel plows, windmills to water cattle, and the railroad. The new technology that makes settlement possible for these pioneers in the plain of Shinar is the invention of bricks. With baked brick and bitumen, they can build a city, and even a tower, in a land without stone.

Third, we know about the desire to be with people of our own kind who speak our language. The citizens of Babel did not want to be scattered across the earth (v. 4). They wanted to live together in their comfortable new hometown. It seems to be human nature to stick with our kind of people. Those who look different or act in different ways make us uncomfortable; and our churches, clubs, and neighborhoods tend to be full of people pretty much like us.

Fourth, we know that unity is powerful. Pulling together, we can achieve our goals and protect ourselves. Mutual understanding and good communication lead to success. In contrast, division and scattering weaken us. Misunderstanding and distance mean that we become strangers rather than fellow citizens. Building a city to keep us together, one strongly defended by a tower, probably makes sense to us.

Fifth, we are familiar with the desire for fame, recognition, and reputation. Cities boast about having the tallest buildings. We erect impressive architecture to perpetuate names and reputations: the Sears Tower, the Washington Monument, or the Taj Mahal. For a biblical example of this human impulse, see 2 Samuel 18:18.

Sixth, we recognize a dangerous side to uncontrolled human potential, advances in technology, and unchecked human aspiration. The text emphasizes the zeal and inventiveness of the people of this new city. An innovative technology of brick making sparks new projects that utilize that technology. But it seems that every new technological discovery has its dangers. New products and processes endanger our environment, our children, even our world. We are incessantly faced with ethical questions posed by new discoveries in medicine and biology. In this story, God recognizes that human inventiveness and determination are becoming a potential problem. Because these humans are concentrated in one place and share a common language, they have become too smart, too competent, and too well organized. The immense power of their social cooperation will lead to unrestrained developments that God is determined to stop. Therefore, God decides that the people of this energetic and progressive storybook city must be scattered.

Seventh, we are well aware that language is a powerful social force and that it has paradoxical potentials that can be used or misused. On the one hand, language is a source of inspiration and action, as it is for the people of this city. Because they can say to each other, "Come, let us...Come, let us" and be understood, they can do new and creative things. However, we also know the frustration of language barriers that can lead to ethnic division and hostility. The fact that we speak different languages plays a major role in ethnic alienation. Many nations experience internal divisions caused by differences in language. History has been blemished by attempts to promote a dominant national language at the expense of less-favored ones.

Step Three: What Is Unfamiliar?

Where are Shinar and Babel? How did those people live? We may not know, but the first readers would have been familiar with Shinar as the wide, flat territory between the Tigris and Euphrates rivers in Mesopotamia (Gen. 10:10). They would have heard travelers' tales about Babel, the ancient city we call Babylon. Readers would know that the mighty cities in that far-off land were built of brick, not the stone so plentiful in Palestine. Perhaps they knew that Mesopotamia was a land of ancient ruins, remnants of vanished civilizations, and of stepped temple towers called ziggurats, built to serve as bridges between heaven and earth.

Ancient cites were not the sprawling webs of highways, neighborhoods, parks, and factories that we envision. Cities held their population tightly in a protective embrace. They were designed for military defense and surrounded by walls. A city might very well have a tower as part of its fortifications (Judg. 8:9; 9:46–49, 51–52; 2 Kings 9:17). The higher this defensive tower, the more secure the city was from attack ("up to heaven," Deut. 1:28; compare Deut. 9:1).

Step Four: Key Words

Earth. The text begins with the phrase "the whole earth had one language," then goes on to describe how "they" migrated. We do not really find out who "they" are until verse 5, when we are informed that these are "mortals, human beings" (see "man in the generic sense" in "Hebrew Word List"). "The whole earth had one language" is a striking phrase, as though Planet Earth itself possessed this one way of speaking. Of course, "earth" can refer either to the surface of the dry land upon which plants, animals, and people live (1:26, 29; 7:3; 8:9; 9:19), or to the people of the earth viewed as a whole (10:25; 18:25; 19:31; 41:57). Here the overlap between *earth* and *humanity* is so prominent that it seems to signal that this story is not only about human beings, but also about humans in relation to the earth as a whole, to Planet Earth. Earth provides a framework around the Babel story, which begins with "the whole earth had one language" and concludes with the confusion of "the language of all the earth."

Earth appears elsewhere as part of the phrase "across the face of the whole/all the earth" (vv. 4, 8, 9). This refers to the earth's surface across which humans move. The horizontal movement of humans spreading out around the earth began with Cain (4:12–16), then continued with population increase "on the face of the ground," (6:1), and after the flood by the expansion of the offspring of Noah (9:19;

10:32). In the Babel story, however, humanity seeks to prevent this spread over the earth through the construction of a city and a tower.

Language. The Hebrew word translated "language" here is literally "lip." It appears five times (vv. 1, 6, 7 [twice, the second time as "speech" in NRSV], 9). This is a somewhat odd usage in that the usual Hebrew word for a language is "tongue." "Lip" implies something like mode or manner of speech, a way of speaking. "Same words" (v. 1) could also be translated "few words." Taken negatively this could refer to an impoverished, childlike vocabulary. Understood positively, this phrase could indicate a straightforward language without cumbersome complexity. "One lip and the same words" is usually understood to mean a shared mother tongue, but could refer to a common *lingua franca* with a restricted but commonly understood set of words used for cooperative projects. In any case, the important thing is that this "one lip" made human cooperation completely transparent and trouble-free.

Word play demonstrates how the structure of language can teach new insights. Instead of *ʾeben* (stone), the people of Shinar discovered how to make *lĕbēnah* (brick); instead of *ḥōmer* (mortar), they used *ḥēmār* (bitumen).

The story does not say in so many words that the result of God's action was a multiplicity of languages. It actually says that God *confused* the language of all the earth with the result that people could no longer understand each other (vv. 7, 9) and that perfect cooperation was prevented. Essentially this tale is more about a universal breakdown in human communication than the origin of different languages. Even so, this breakdown appears most clearly in the reality of diverse languages, and so this story may be taken as an etiology for them.

One. The key word *one* is used not only of having one language, but also of being one people (v. 6). If we look carefully, we can see that there are two things going on here, a minor plot and a major one. In the minor plot, God confuses the one language so that cooperation becomes impossible and the city gets the name Babel, "confusion." However, the main weight of the story is on a parallel train of events. Humanity is one people and wants to stay that way. Therefore, they build a city to prevent dispersal and to gain a name. To prevent even further human projects that will violate what God wants to see happening, God scatters them and they stop building the city.

There. The little word *there* is repeated five times—in verses 2, 7, and 8, and twice in verse 9. The author seems to want us to focus on that particular geographical location in the land of Shinar and to see that God's actions are directed against humanity's attempt to remain settled in that one particular spot.

Bricks. Construction with bricks is the technological achievement that makes this city building project possible by overcoming a lack of stone and mortar. The people first decide to fabricate bricks for construction and only then decide exactly what to build. Israelite readers would have considered brick to be an exotic building material and thought of it as a (perhaps inferior) substitute for stone (Isa. 9:10). Bricks were unnecessary in Palestine, which had plenty of stone for building. Making brick required more political organization than using stone, and such communal cooperation was characteristic of Mesopotamia's urban civilization.

City. In Mesopotamian thought, cities had originated through actions taken by both gods and humans. In Genesis, by contrast, only humans are responsible for the development of cities (4:17; 10:10–12). In the ancient world cities were viewed as protective containers for their populations. They were enclosures of tight social cooperation, the innovators and guardians of civilization. Cities concentrated human potential. Their dense populations and high frequency of interaction would have led to countless inventive conversations such as, "Come let us make bricks." The city was already an ancient institution by the time Israel emerged into history. Cities provided cultural continuity over the centuries. Some cities, such as Babylon, had endured for generations and were famous in the sense that their names were widely known (compare "let us make a name," v. 4). In every way, the city was the polar opposite of the dispersal that these first humans are seeking to avoid.

Tower. The repeated word *tower* is certainly important and has captured the imagination of readers over centuries. We are not told of this tower's purpose. Is it is to be a temple tower like the ziggurats of Babylon, or a fortification tower? As a ziggurat, it would be an exotic touch like the bricks and bitumen, describing unfamiliar life in a far-off place. However, the Israelite readers would have been much more familiar with defensive towers. The tower was so much a part of the concept of a city that the Hebrew word for tower (*migdol*) was part of the name of some Israelite towns (Josh. 15:37; 19:38). Jerusalem was noted for its impressive fortification towers (Ps. 48:12; 122:7).

In both its occurrences, the word *tower* is paired with *city*, so that the combination "a city and a tower" sounds like a single expression.

Let us build, not just any ordinary city, but a specially powerful one, a "city-with-tower." The tower is not really the center of attention. It is never spoken of alone but only in connection with the city (vv. 4, 5). Then the tower drops out, and the city alone becomes the focus. Construction on the city stops, but nothing is said about the tower (v. 8).

In Isaiah 14:13–14, the king of historical Babylon is condemned for his boastful assault on heaven. Are we intended to understand this tower of Babel (Babylon) as an overconfident attempt to reach up to heaven and invade God's realm? Strong arguments oppose this interpretation. The text does not mention an assault on the divine realm. The only statement of what is wrong with the tower is that it is a sign that soon nothing will be impossible for cooperative, inventive humans. The tower is a symptom of the potential problems inherent in too much human collaboration.

That its top is planned to be "in the heavens" seems to be a way of saying it will be "sky-high," that is to say, the tallest tower imaginable. Like our own sky*scrapers,* this tower is intended to touch the sky from the perspective of those who view it. The translation "heavens" is misleading, since it induces us to think in terms of the realm of God from which God descends (vv. 5, 7). A better translation in this context would be "sky," that is to say, the dome stretched out over the earth across which birds fly (Gen. 1:7–8; 20). That the LORD has to go down "to see the city and the tower" (v. 5) indicates that this puny tower never even gets close to threatening God's realm. God's reaction is specifically intended to prevent future developments and to scatter humanity. Nothing is said about defending heaven against any human onslaught.

Is this Babylonian tower presented as a sign of human arrogance? This would still be possible even if no actual assault on heaven were implied. Cities fortified with high fortifications and lofty towers appear several times in the Bible as poetic images of overweening pride deserving of destruction (Isa. 2:12–15; 30:25; Jer. 51:53; Ezek. 26:4, 9). Moreover, the city of Babylon was a byword for arrogance (Isa. 13:19; Jer. 51:41), and the prophets celebrated its fall and destruction (Isa. 21:9; Jer. 51:6–14, 41–44). Ultimately, we cannot be certain that Babel's sky-high tower implies arrogance. What cannot be questioned, however, is that this tower is subordinated to the more important image of the city. As an urban defensive structure, the tower strengthens the image of this city as a protective enclosure for its inhabitants, one that can prevent them from being scattered and bring them fame.

Come, let us. This phrase occurs three times. In verses 3 and 4, it emphasizes the parallel between the two successive human cooperative projects, first bricks, then a city. The double summons communicates zeal and eagerness. In verse 7, the same phrase describes God's counter reaction to these developments.

Name. The city is intended to prevent scattering by providing its inhabitants with a name. Name means not only recognition and reputation, but also a unifying group identity that can hold them together as a single people. There is irony in this. They get a name (v. 9; *šēm*, "Hebrew Word List"), but it turns out to be Babel *(bābel),* taken to be a pun on *bālal,* meaning confusion (see the NRSV note). Babel is the ordinary Hebrew designation for Babylon, the name we have inherited from the Greeks. This pun critiques and insults Babylon, suggesting that it is not really Babel (the gate of God) but Balal, the home of confusion. The words "name" *(šēm)* and "there" *(šām)* also work together to create wordplay. They sought to achieve a name there (vv. 2, 4), but now the city is named Babel "because there the LORD confused...and from there the LORD scattered" (v. 9).

Scatter. This key word appears in verses 4, 8, and 9. Both settlement in Shinar and building a tower-city are attempts to prevent scattering (vv. 2, 4). The unity of human language also helps prevent this. In the context of Genesis, God wants the earth to be populated (1:28; 9:1), but the concentration of population into a single city blocks God's plan. God's actions move in two directions, confusing language (vv. 7, 9a) and scattering the people (vv. 8, 9b). However, both actions lead to the same result: humans are spread "over the face of the earth" (vv. 8, 9). The pre-flood situation of population expansion "on the face of the earth" (6:1) is restored. Because ethnic unity and mutually comprehensible language are necessary requirements for the sort of cooperation that made possible the planning and building of the city (v. 6), scattering and language confusion go hand in hand. The two divine actions are woven tightly together in verses 7–9.

Come down/go down. Did you notice that God descends to earth twice, first to see the city and tower (v. 5) and then to confuse language (v. 7)? This repetition is a bit confusing in itself! There is some humor in verse 5. The tower was planned to be sky-high, but God has to go down to be able to see it.

Step Five: Opposites and Contrasts

The story opens with an opposition. Humans are *migrating,* but then they *settle* down. They seek to counter the possibility of being scattered in three ways:

- settlement in one place
- building a permanent city, complete with tower
- questing for a reputation

Horizontal elements such as migration "from the east," "plain," and scattering "over the face of all the earth" play off against *vertical* elements such as the tower and God's descent from above. The tower goes up; God comes down.

Several of the opposites in this story line up into "before" and "after" categories. Human circumstances and human plans make up the "before" situation. The results of God's action constitute the state of affairs "after."

- "One language and the same words" (v. 1) in contrast to "not understand one another's speech" (v. 7)
- "The whole earth had one language" (v. 1) in opposition to "confused the language of all the earth" (v. 9)
- "A plain in the land of Shinar" (v. 2) versus "abroad over the face of all the earth" (v. 9)
- "Settled there" (v. 2) contrasting with "from there the LORD scattered" (v. 9)
- "A name for ourselves" (v. 4) in distinction to "it was called Babel" (v. 9)

The story sounds like an illustration of the proverb: "The human mind plans the way, / but the LORD directs the steps" (Prov. 16:9).

Step Six: Characters

One has to feel a certain sympathy for and attraction to these new *migrants.* Who wouldn't want to settle down in a permanent home and build themselves a nice city? They have impressive capabilities. They are inventive. They can build even without stone and mortar because they can talk out their plans and ideas. As competent builders, they work out their techniques first, make their plans, and envision the outcome before they start construction. Without doubt, one would think, their name will be known universally as the people who constructed such an amazing city and lofty tower. Like

Man and Woman standing before the tree of knowledge (3:5–6), they are on the threshold of even greater new achievements. Once again, however, God intervenes.

The *junior gods* of God's heavenly administration make up another set of story characters. God addresses them as "us" (as in Gen. 3:22) and invites them to descend to earth. Apparently, they go down to have some hand in confusing language and scattering the world's population.

God, too, is a character in this drama. Unlimited human potential is a problem for God. Although we are never told exactly why, context suggests that God's plans to have humanity populate the whole world would be undermined by concentrated and permanent settlement in the plain of Shinar. In addition, the prediction that "nothing...will now be impossible" (v. 7) hints that future human projects could be detrimental to other plans God may have and perhaps even hazardous to the earth itself. Repeated references to the "earth" (vv. 1, 4, 8, 9) suggest that it is just as important to the story as the humans are.

Repeating what happened in Eden, humanity seems once again to be getting too close to what it means to be "like God." It is instructive that Job defines God in terms that echo what is said here about talented humanity: "I know that you can do all things, / and that no purpose of yours can be thwarted" (Job 42:2). Certainly we post-Holocaust, post-Hiroshima, post-Chernobyl readers cannot hear the words "this is only the beginning of what they will do" without a shudder.

Step Seven: Patterns and Structures

The story uses a language of totality to indicate that this is a foundational event with universal consequences. It involves the *whole earth* or *all the earth* (the same expression in Hebrew; vv. 1, 4, 8, twice in v. 9). Humans have *all* one language, and (literally) "it will not be impossible from them, *all* which they propose to do" (v. 6).

The phrase *whole earth/all the earth* forms a frame around the whole story, occurring nearly at the beginning of verse 1 and at the end of verse 9. Another roughly overlapping framework is produced by the reversal of "whole earth...language" in verse 1 into "language... of all the earth" in verse 9a. The repetition of *all the earth* in verse 9 links the corresponding actions of confusing and scattering and hammers home the decisiveness of God's response.

An example of delayed exposition occurs when readers are not immediately told the identity of the indefinite "they" in verse 2 until they are described as "mortals" in verse 5 (that is, "sons of ʾādām").

Several narrative gaps appear. We are not told why the humans are so worried about being scattered. The actual act of building is never described, but only assumed in verse 5. It is unclear whether they ever complete the city (compare v. 5 with v. 8).

Verses 3 and 4 are nicely balanced. Repeated speeches describe a two-stage process: first the development of materials and technology, then plans for the building project itself. Repetition of "we" and "us" emphasizes that this is a purely human project. It will be accomplished for purely human purposes: "build *ourselves* a city...make a name for *ourselves*." In Hebrew, verse 3 is a balanced poetic couplet:

and there was for them / brick / as stone
and bitumen / was for them / as mortar

Verse 4 measures out information about the construction plan bit by bit: a city—and a tower—which will be a high one—and make a name—lest we be scattered.

Verse 6 uses repetition effectively. The repetition of "one people" and "one language" in the first part of verse 6 reminds the reader of the situation laid out in verse 1. In the second part of verse 6, this seemingly neutral situation is reinterpreted as a problem through the repetition of *do*: "they will do" and "they propose to do."

God's actions in verses 8 and 9 are framed by reversed repetition (in Hebrew word order):

the Lord scattered them abroad / from there /
    over the face of all the earth
from there / the Lord scattered them abroad /
    over the face of all the earth

Step Eight: Plot Movement

The story of the tower of Babel is carefully crafted and artistically formed. The plot is straightforward. It moves from an *exposition* of background (v. 1) to the unfolding of the *problem* (vv. 2–4), then to the measures God's takes to *resolve* the problem (vv. 5–8), and finally to a *summary* of God's actions and their results (v. 9).

A carefully balanced, *two-part structure* shows that God's response to humanity's actions was judicious and appropriate. Humanity's exploits are presented in verses 1–4; then God takes the initiative in verses 5–9, reacting to what humans have done. The two halves of the story are almost mirror images of each other. Human actions are reflected by God's reactions:

v. 1 one language, the same words / v. 6 one people, one language
v. 3 come let us / v. 7 come let us
v. 4 come let us build a city / v. 8 they left off building the city
v. 4 make a name / v. 8 it was called Babel
v. 4 we shall be scattered / vv. 8, 9 scattered them

Verse 5 serves as the crossover point or hinge, recounting God's descent (v. 5a), but also referring to the human action of building (v. 5b). The two halves are so strictly compartmentalized that no verbal interaction takes place between God and humanity (in contrast to the stories of Eden and Cain).

Thus the text creates a fitting balance between human action and divine reaction, while at the same time God's response reverses human purposes. People build so that they will not be scattered (v. 4), but God scatters them so they must leave off building (v. 8). Common language means cooperation (v. 3), but God confuses language so they do not understand (v. 7). They seek a famous name (v. 4) and end up with an infamous one (v. 8).

The three parallel speeches beginning "come, let us" coordinate the two halves of the plot. In verses 3 and 4, humans use their unity of language to encourage each other in their plans to avoid being scattered and stay together in one place. In verse 7, God incorporates the junior level deities in plans to confound that unity of language and scatter the humans from that one place.

The two themes of language confusion and dispersal interlock so tightly that they cannot be separated. Confusion in language is prepared for by verse 1 ("one language") and dispersal by verse 2 ("settled there"). The city as an achievement in cooperation points to confusion; the city as a way to make a famous name points to dispersal. God's proposal to confuse in verse 7 leads directly to God's action to disperse in verse 8. Although language confusion is intended to quash questionable human schemes (v. 6), it is actually dispersal that terminates the city building project (v. 8). Finally, verse 9 summarizes the two themes side by side. The city is Babel because of confusion, but is also the center from which God scatters humanity. Apparently, we are intended to understand that confusion served as a secondary mechanism by which God achieved the primary goal of dispersal.

Step Nine: Purpose and Intention

As is true of other stories in Genesis, this narrative takes us from primeval circumstances to the conditions of present-day life. Verse 1 represents *then*, and verse 9 describes *now*. Once upon a time an era of ideal human communication and cooperation existed in a single community at a single place. Now our language communications are muddled, and we live in diverse communities around the world. The human situation changed from *then* to *now* through a combination of human aspirations and God's reaction to them.

"Therefore" (v. 9; compare 2:25) shows that to some degree the story is intended to provide an explanation for the name Babylon. It may also seek to explain why this city was famous for its monumental temple tower. Remember that Babylon would have been a living, and often hostile, city for Israelite readers, not an unfinished ruin. There is a certain anti-Babylon flavor in the insulting connection of Babel with confusion.

The story explains our inability to understand what other humans say. It answers the question, "Why, in spite of our common descent from Noah's sons, do we speak different languages?" As we have already noted, however, some caution is in order at this point. The text does not quite say that God produced different languages, only that that God confused language so that understanding became impossible.

Step Ten: Text in Context

This story begins with humanity as a single entity, and thus does not take into account the Table of Nations in Genesis 10 or the distinction of languages already described in 10:5. One could say that it backtracks and zooms in on 10:25, the point in time when humanity was divided.

A number of themes from previous stories are continued and repeated. The Babel episode describes a further stage in the growth and maturation of the human race. Growing up began in Eden, and Man and Woman were forced to leave it behind. Now humanity's opened eyes and knowledge of good and evil seem to have achieved new levels. Just as humans could not stay in Eden's nursery but were forced out into the adult world, so now God refuses to let them settle down into their new urban paradise in Shinar.

Scattering over the whole earth culminates an epic journey of human expansion that began with Adam, Eve, and Cain (3:23–24; 4:16), continued in the population upsurge before the flood (6:1), then started again when Noah's sons left the ark to populate the earth (9:18–19). The locale or direction "east" helps tie some of these movements together (2:8; 3:24; 4:16; 11:2).

A theme of progressive alienation also continues. This began with estrangement between wife and husband and then brothers. In the story of Noah's sons, it spreads to a breakdown between parent and child. Now an inability to understand one another's speech alienates the speakers of one language from one another.

Finally, this story circles back to the subject of God's reaction to dangerous human potentials. Humans gained knowledge and became something like gods, so God blocked access to Eden lest they live forever (3:23). Humans intermarried with minor deities and produced offspring, so God limited their life span (6:3). God reacted to human wickedness with a flood (6:5). Now once again increasing human maturity and talent produce capacities and aspirations that collide with God's designs. Like Cain, these humans build a city; and like Cain's children, they invent new ways of doing things (4:17, 20–22). This new stage in human development provokes God to a preemptive strike to avoid dangerous future problems inherent in human abilities.

Step Eleven: Claims and Assertions

This story is a warning. Grand human projects may overstep what God wants to see happen, and apparently noble human aspirations may run counter to God's plans. God is willing to take aggressive action to obstruct any human plans and potentials that run counter to God's agenda. The height of Babel's tower, so impressive from our human perspective but so puny from God's viewpoint, calls attention to the unbridgeable distance between heaven and earth.

The Babel story claims that God cares enough about humanity to exercise what we might call "tough love." Humans were to fill the earth, but could never fulfill God's plan while remaining cooped up in a single city, building their little tower. God scattered them across the earth, bringing about exactly what they had feared all along. This suggests that there will be times when the new realities God sends into our lives will realize our worst fears and seem hurtful, tough, and overly demanding.

Moreover, God cares enough to set limits for us. We need to be protected from the dangerous consequences of our great talents. We may have foolhardy and dangerous plans to build appalling new war machines, or destroy the soil and the forests and the oceans, or play Dr. Frankenstein in our labs. Perhaps we will discover that God is not willing to let us destroy Planet Earth or ourselves by allowing us to cooperate in accomplishing such projects. Perhaps new obstacles will arise to prevent earth's over-clever children from playing our dangerous little games. Perhaps the misunderstandings, confusions, and mix-ups caused by our linguistic and national diversities are not all bad, but God's way of undermining dangerous human cooperation and limiting our perilous experiments.

Again, God clearly wants us to grow up. God is not willing to let us stay in our little homogeneous, uniform, comfortable worlds. We may feel snug and cozy when we interact with people who look just like us, sound just like us, and think just like us. But the Babel story implies that God has a penchant for sending us opportunities to meet up with people who look and sound and think in ways very different from what we are used to. Humanity has branched out into an immense variety of different races, cultures, languages, and customs, and apparently God wants us to experience and appreciate these.

Interpreters from the non-Western world often see the picture of a "one-language world" and a centralizing fortress city as a negative and oppressive development. This city is, after all, none other than Babylon, a biblical symbol for tyranny and oppression. Imperial or colonial rulers have often imposed a repressive unity of language upon indigenous peoples. Viewed from this perspective, God is doing something beneficial for humanity by breaking down a monolithic linguistic unity and breaking up a mono-cultural totalitarianism. Forcing humanity to develop into a rich variety of scattered peoples is an act of grace, not of punishment. God's intention for humanity is diversity, not imposed uniformity, and a multiplicity of emancipated peoples rather than the domination of a single political structure. In her Magnificat, Mary reminds us that scattering can be a good thing. God is at work to turn the world's relationships of power and wealth upside down and "has scattered the proud in the thoughts of their hearts" (Luke 1:51).

Sources

English has made the proper name *Babel* into a common noun meaning "a scene of confusion" or "confused sounds." *Babel* (usually with a long "a") has been enriched (or confused) in our consciousness by its resemblance to the unrelated word *babble* (short "a") meaning "foolish chatter, childish or imperfect efforts at speech."

For structural analysis I drew on Ellen van Would, *Words Become Worlds: Semantic Studies of Genesis 1–11*, Biblical Interpretation Series 6 (Leiden: Brill, 1994), 84–109, and J. P. Fokkelman, *Narrative Art in Genesis: Specimens of Stylistic and Structural Analysis,* SSN 17 (Assen: Van Gorcum, 1975), 11–45. I also used Peter J. Harland, "Vertical or Horizontal: The Sin of Babel," *VT* 48 (1998): 515–33.

For an ecological reading, see Ellen van Wolde, "The Earth Story as Presented by the Tower of Babel Narrative," in *The Earth Story in Genesis,* The Earth Bible 2, ed. Norman C. Habel and Shirley Wurst (Sheffield: Sheffield Academic Press, 2000), 147–57. For non-Western interpretations, consult *Return to Babel: Global Perspectives on the Bible,* ed. J. Levison and P. Pope-Levison (Louisville: Westminster John Knox Press, 1999), 13–33.

CHAPTER 9

From Eden to Babel and Beyond

These stories deal with the fundamentals of human existence and humanity's relationship to God. What does it mean to be human? What are we like? What are our problems and strengths? They explore the growth of human maturity, but also human resistance to God's will and the tragedies that result. Humanity cannot stay in Eden, for God drives them from there into the real world. Nor can humanity stay settled in Babel, for God scatters them from there to spread over all the earth. Humanity's epic journey begins with God's observation that "the man has become like one of us" and resumes when God judges that "nothing that they propose to do will now be impossible."

Finding Unity

Whoever gathered and organized these originally independent narratives linked them together so that they move forward in time and outward in space. Expanding family descent produces movement in time. Lineage sequences run within the stories themselves. The first line leads to the foundation of civilization but lapses into violence: Adam and Eve to Cain to Lamech (Gen. 4:1–2, 18). A second line carries on past the flood to Babel: Adam and Eve to Seth to Noah to his sons to the peopling of the "whole earth" (4:25–26; 6:8; 9:18–19; 11:8–9). Genealogies also come between the stories in Genesis 5 and 10. The combined effect unifies the narratives into a temporal sequence.

Expansion in space provides a second unifying factor. The stories begin with humans in one place, in Eden in the east (2:8, 15), but they are driven away from there (3:22–24). Cain becomes a wanderer, driven away from the ground (4:12–13), and settles "east of Eden" (4:16). The human population grows (6:1). Noah and his sons set forth from the ark to populate the "whole earth" (9:18–19). The "whole earth" moves "from the east" (11:1–2) and settles in one city, but Yahweh scatters them from there so they are dispersed far and wide (11:8–9).

An All-encompassing Etiology

These stories form a grand etiology that explains how we humans got to where we are today. They are about the whole human race (Gen. 2–3; 6:1–8); all nomads, musicians, and smiths (4:20–22); and the whole earth (9:19; 11:1). These narratives describe humanity's step-by-step development from the situations of the prehistoric past to the circumstances of our present-day world. To some extent, this process consists of movement from one state of being to its contrasting opposite. Genesis 2–3 depicts our development from nakedness to clothing, from potential immortality to mortality, from childlike naiveté to adult sexual awareness, and from being the children of our parents to becoming spouses and parents ourselves. Genesis 4 tells how the role of brother was transformed first into that of rival and then into that of victim. In the opening verses of Genesis 6, the opposing categories of godhood versus humanity and spirit versus flesh are resolved by the imposition of our present limited life span. In the story of Noah's sons, the kinship categories of brother and nephew degenerate into the socially oppressive categories of master and slave. Finally, Genesis 11 plays off city and community over against dispersal and ethnicity. Limitations on the human condition slowly build up: on being like God, on unlimited revenge, on life span, on social equality, and on the cooperative power of language.

The driving question of etiology is, "Why are things different now than they must have once been when the world was a simpler, less complicated place?" There must have been a time when there was no shame, fear of snakes, clothing, jealousy, murder, blood vengeance, or cities. The logic of etiology is one of irreversible "before and after" situations. The stories from Eden to Babel are set in a special era of the time "before":

- "the day that the LORD God made" (2:4)
- "naked, and were not ashamed" (2:25)
- "he was the ancestor of those who…" (4:20, 21)
- "began to invoke the name" (4:26)
- "people began to multiply" (6:1)
- "in those days" (6:4)
- "first to plant a vineyard" (9:20)
- "one language and the same words" (11:1)

Often the etiological logic is left implicit for the reader to discern, but sometimes the connections between "before" and "now" is spelled out:
- "therefore a man leaves" (2:24)
- "he shall rule over you" (3:16)
- "those who live in tents/play the lyre" (4:20, 21)
- "their days shall be one hundred twenty years" (6:3)
- "let Canaan be his slave" (9:26, 27)
- "confused the language" (11:9)

Human nature assumes that the past was a golden age and that our present is worse than our original situation. So these stories move from the ease of garden life to the frustrations and scarcities of subsistence farming, from "one flesh" equality to sexism, from brotherhood to murderous reprisal, from equality to slavery, and from cooperation to miscommunication. One thing is clear, though. That earlier situation of the time before is no longer available to us. The way back to Eden is permanently blocked off. The world's peoples can no longer say to each other, "Come, let us make bricks," and expect to be understood.

Yet the tone of these stories is not one of despair. We have lost much, surely, but at the same time much has been gained. We cling to each other in the joy of marriage (2:23–24) and have children (3:20; 4:1–2, 17, 25). Now there are cities, occupations and crafts, music, wine, technology, and multiculturalism (4:17, 20–22; 9:20; 11:3, 8–9). There is religion (4:3–4, 26).

Shared Themes

The Ground and the Earth

For centuries, Christians and Jews have read the early chapters of Genesis from a human-oriented perspective, as though human beings were the only parties affected by what is said to have taken place. Actually, however, these narratives insist that the ground and the earth have been repeatedly impacted by human behavior. Genesis 2 starts with a problem involving the *ground*, which lacks someone to till it (2:5), and Genesis 3 concludes with the solution to that problem in the shape of the humans who go forth "to till the ground" (3:23). Humanity has an intimate relationship with the ground. We are formed from it (2:7), put in a garden produced from it (2:9), eat of it (3:17), decompose in it (3:19), till it (4:2; 9:20), pollute it with violence and are alienated from it (4:10–12, 14), multiply across it (6:1), and are blotted out from it (6:7). The association between *earth* and humanity is likewise intimate and concrete. God made us on earth, and our wickedness escalated in it (6:5, 6). We wander over earth (4:14), populate it (9:19), and spread out across it (11:4, 8, 9). At one point, humanity is even identified with earth (11:1). An obvious conclusion is that God's plans and activities are not only about us. God cares about Planet Earth and its soil. We are part of Earth's destiny and not independent tyrants over it.

Human Nature and Transgression

These are narratives of repeated human failure and God's responses to those failures. Indeed, this can be seen as the fundamental pattern of human existence. Human beings make bad choices or get involved in suspect situations: eating from the tree (3:6), murder (4:8), problematic sex (6:2), evil inclinations (6:5), shaming a parent (9:22), and seeking to avoid dispersal (11:4). Sometimes God reacts by becoming involved in dialog with the humans or by internalized speech. God interrogates and chides the first couple and Cain (3:9–13; 4:9–11), but in later stories decides things internally or speaks to the minor deities (6:3, 7; 11:6–7). There are negative consequences (3:14–19, 22–24; 4:12, 16; 6:3, 7; 9:25; 11:8–9). However, God mitigates these negative consequences three times, by making clothes (3:21), by giving Cain a protective mark (4:15), and by taking note of Noah (6:8). In these stories, humans undermine what God has established, but God protects them from at least some of the consequences of their actions. Moreover, sometimes what seem to be negative consequences turn out to be positive steps. This is clearest in the Babel story, where dispersal counteracts the human desire to stagnate as one people in one place, in conflict with God's plan for them to populate the earth.

God plays no role in the story of Noah's sons. Slavery is presented as a purely human decision, without divine approval or input. The cycle of wrongdoing and consequences sometimes operates on a purely human plane, without any need for divine intervention.

The Mystery of God

These stories trace God's emerging reactions to human actions and the human exercise of free choice. God is presented as mysterious, gracious, and determined to manage a situation that seems to be spinning out of control.

First, God remains an enigma. God mysteriously sets up the arena for human choice by placing the tree of knowledge in a prominent place, by prohibiting it without providing much of an explanation, and by creating Snake as a crafty animal. God regards Abel's sacrifice and disregards Cain's without stating a reason. God seeks to blot out life on earth with a flood, but immediately undermines this plan by choosing Noah.

Second, God is gracious. Observing that the original situation of Man was not good, God furnishes the world with animals and Woman. God graciously provides the first humans with clothing and Cain with protection. God conscientiously warns Cain about the dangers he faces. God evidences an emotional attachment to these humans and is deeply troubled by the need to destroy them. God chooses Noah.

Finally, God seeks to keep feisty and problematic humans under some kind of control. Humans have their own perceptions and make their own decisions. They are prey to attacks by the sin monster (4:7) and the sexual advances of heavenly beings (6:2). "Every inclination" of their heart is evil (6:5), and "nothing that they propose to do" seems impossible (11:6). In response, God blocks off immortality for humans, who have come too close to being like gods. God claims control over retributive vengeance against Cain, although Lamech asserts a right to take massive retaliation into his own hands. God limits human life span to minimize the danger posed by a volatile mixture of the divine and human spheres. At one point, it seems as though endemic wickedness can no longer be controlled but must be exterminated by a flood; however, God permits life to go on. God cancels out human attempts to stagnate in one place as one people.

Renouncing Eden, Forsaking Babel

Humanity grows up, first as a pair of individuals in Eden, then as a species. Perhaps the tower city of Babel can be seen as humanity's attempt to build a second Eden, a protective enclosure designed to prevent scattering out into the wider world. Gardens and cities are similar (Lam. 2:6). Water is important to both (Ps. 46:4; Ezek. 47:1–12). Walls protect them from outside dangers (Song 4:12).

God's reaction to the tower city of Babel is much like God's response to transgression in Eden. In each story, God addresses the junior deities of God's administrative council before taking decisive action (3:22; 11:7). In this way, these actions are presented as very serious decisions, like those that a human ruler would take in council. The danger in Eden is that humans might achieve immortality. The danger at Babel is that humans will never grow beyond their present narrow linguistic and cultural uniformity and never populate the earth. God responds to each crisis in a similar way. God "sent [humans] forth from the garden" (3:23); "from there the LORD scattered them abroad" (11:9).

Baby birds sometimes need to be pushed out of the nest so they are forced to learn to fly. Perhaps we are being told that God drove humanity from both Eden and Babel so that we could come of age. Yearning to return to Eden is unrealistic. We have outgrown kindergarten and are no longer babes in the wood. Moreover, a flaming sword and fearsome cherubim guard the way back. In the same way, yearning to achieve some sort of mono-cultural unity without ethnic or linguistic diversity is equally fallacious, even dangerous. Political tyrants, religious triumphalists, and racial supremacists may seek a return to the monochromatic, mono-linguistic walled tower city. It seems that God wants us to enjoy a rainbow of linguistic diversity and cultural variety.